In Walt We Trust

In Walt We Trust

*How a Queer Socialist Poet Can
Save America from Itself*

★

JOHN MARSH

MONTHLY REVIEW PRESS

New York

Copyright © 2015 by John Marsh
All Rights Reserved
Library of Congress Cataloging-in-Publication Data

Marsh, John, 1975–
  In Walt We Trust : How a Queer Socialist Poet Can Save America from
Itself
/ John Marsh.
     pages cm
  Includes bibliographical references and index.
  ISBN 978-1-58367-475-8 (hardback)
  1. Whitman, Walt, 1819–1892—Appreciation. 2. Whitman, Walt,
1819–1892—Influence. 3. Influence (Literary, artistic, etc.) 4. Conduct
of life in literature. I. Title.
  PS3231.M186 2015
  811'.3—dc23

                      2014050291

Monthly Review Press
146 West 29th Street, Suite 6W
New York, New York 10001
www.monthlyreview.org

5 4 3 2 1

Contents

To Nora Fitzgerald Marsh

Acknowledgments

Thanks to John Christman, Melissa Flashman,
Chad Lavin, Carole Marsh, Mike Marsh, Benjamin
Schreier, Erica Stevens, Michael Yates, and most of all
to Debra Hawhee, still my first reader, best reader.

A Note on Editions of Whitman's Poems

Depending on how you count, Walt Whitman published six or seven editions of *Leaves of Grass*, making additions, deletions, and changes along the way, rarely for the better. These multiple editions make citing poems more difficult than usual. Unless noted, I cite the text of the poem as it originally appeared. I also retain Whitman's original punctuation, including his various forms of ellipses, which should not be read to indicate omitted text. With one or two exceptions, I give the title that Whitman ultimately bestowed on the poems, and by which they became known. For example, when discussing "Song of Myself," I cite the original 1855 version of the poem, and I refer to the poem as "Song of Myself," even though Whitman only gave it that title in the 1881–82 edition. Similarly, I cite the 1856 version of "Crossing Brooklyn Ferry," the edition in which it first appeared, even though Whitman gave it that title in the 1860 edition. In the 1856 edition, it appeared as "Sun-Down Poem."

In general, I have relied on two collections of Whitman's poems: The Library of America's *Complete Poetry and Collected Prose*, which reprints the original 1855 *Leaves of Grass*, the 1891–92 deathbed edition, and the 1892 *Complete Prose Works*; and Gary Schmidgall's *Walt Whitman: Selected Poems 1855–1892*, which reprints most of the poems as they originally appeared in the various editions. References are always to page numbers.

Walt Whitman—A Poetic Comfort

Is he beloved long and long after he is buried? Does the young
man think often of him? and the young woman think often of
him? and do the middleaged and the old think of him?
—WALT WHITMAN, "Preface" to *Leaves of Grass* (1855)

O n the night of July 15, 1979, Jimmy Carter sat down
in the Oval Office, stared soulfully into the television
camera, and delivered one of the most honest, passion-
ate, and imprudent speeches in American history. Carter began by
outlining the problems Americans currently faced: an economic
recession, spiraling inflation, unemployment, and, most urgently,
energy shortages and gas lines. He argued, however, that "the
true problems of our Nation are much deeper." Sounding more
like an existential philosopher than a president, Carter observed
that Americans had more and more doubts about the meaning
of their lives, and less and less faith in a unity of purpose for the
nation. What ailed America, he said, was "a crisis of confidence,"
a "crisis that strikes at the very heart and soul and spirit of our
national will."

Carter sympathized with ordinary Americans in their moment
of crisis, but he did not let them off the hook. In the most con-
troversial part of his speech, he charged that "in a nation that

was proud of hard work, close-knit communities, and our faith in God, too many of us now tend to worship self-indulgence and consumption."

Although Carter never used the word, newspapers quickly dubbed the whole effort his "malaise" speech.[1] On its thirtieth anniversary in 2009, a contemporary historian called it "one of the worst speeches in the history of the presidency."[2]

Perhaps. Today, though, Carter's speech seems more relevant—and needed—than ever, especially as the United States suffers from another crisis of confidence and wallows in another bout of malaise. We do not have gas lines or rampant inflation, but otherwise America circa 2015 looks a lot like America circa 1979. Then, as now, the United States wanders in the shadow of an economic recession. Then, as now, Americans have lost faith in their government. True, unlike then, we do not face an immediate energy crisis, but we do face an even graver long-term one in global warming. And if Carter thought that Americans in 1979 worshipped self-indulgence and consumption, what might he make of our bookmarked pornography sites, our McMansions, or Black Friday, the annual holy day we set aside for shopping?

When it comes to malaise, that vague awareness of moral and social decline, the 1970s have nothing on us.

I know because I had been given a fair share of it myself. From the outside, I could not look more content: good job, happy marriage, adorable daughter, even a loyal dog. All was not well, though, despite the outward prosperity. I had reservations about having a child, which never entirely went away despite the fact that our daughter grew more lovely and cheerful nearly every day of her life. I also doubted whether my profession—teaching college students literature—did anyone any good, or if it was not, as our campus and our culture seemed to insist more and more, and louder and louder, a frivolous, luxurious diversion, like sailing or chamber music, that an austere, hardheaded nation could no longer afford. After all, if it could not get you a job, or "grow" the economy, what good was it?

Worse, in my late twenties, I started getting relentless, disabling headaches. They would linger for days at a time, occasionally for a week or longer, pounding away at my temples and leaving the left side of my face numb. As I aged into my thirties, the headaches came more often. They consumed my life. I spent most of my time trying to get rid of them, and the rest of my time monitoring myself for new ones. The daily medication I took, a generic antidepressant, did little for the headaches but, on the bright side, did give me horror-show nightmares. And because even a whiff of alcohol would bring on a headache, I gave up drinking, which probably did me good in the long run, given how much I drank and how much comfort I found in it, but now in the short term left me dreadfully sober.

None of these maladies compares with losing a job, losing a loved one, or losing your health—although the headaches felt like a serious enough attack on the country of my health. But together these woes often made daily life seem more like a chore than a blessing. When my neurologist looked me in the eyes and asked me if I had thoughts of suicide, I lied and said no.

Less personally, and in Carter's terms, I suffered from fully-grown doubts, not just growing doubts, about the meaning of life and the purpose of our country.

As for our country, its purpose seemed to be to make a handful of people fabulously wealthy while locking everyone else into a life of economic insecurity. In the wake of the recession of 2008, unemployment reached levels not seen since the Great Depression, and more children lived in poverty than had in generations. Yet little was done, or even proposed, to repair either of these quiet disasters, except to wait and hope, and so, not surprisingly, even after the recession technically ended, they continued.[3] Even before the Great Recession, income inequality had approached levels not seen since the 1920s, and here, too, little was done, and even less proposed, to correct the great and growing divide between the rich and everyone else.[4] Meanwhile, our president, who had campaigned the first time around on hope and the second time around on being the lesser of two evils, had mostly disappointed, not least because (to those of us on the political left, anyway) one of our two major political parties had been captured by reactionaries who wanted to turn the clock back to the 1950s, except when it came to taxes and the safety net, when only the 1890s would do.

As for the meaning of life, nothing leaped out. As a run-of-the-mill atheist, and someone passingly acquainted with contemporary science, I had answers to all of the big questions that are supposed to keep us up at night. Yes, our universe is merely an accident. No, there is no design, no purpose. Yes, every life is irrelevant. However, the disturbing thing about these questions was not the settled answers, but how little the answers mattered. In truth, they did not keep us up at night, because what good would it do to worry about such juvenile things? We were serious people, with lives to lead, and serious people with lives to lead did not worry that everything could just as easily have never existed and, since you will soon enough not exist, it does not matter whether it ever existed or not. No, the less said about such things the better. But just because we did not mention these doubts about the purpose of life in polite company, or in any company, or even to ourselves, that did not mean they did not, from time to time, cast a pall over our lives, as well they should.

To put it briefly, Jimmy Carter may or may not have been right to diagnose a crisis of confidence in Americans of 1979. Today, though, the diagnosis fits me and, I think, many other Americans just about perfectly. When it comes to our jobs, our mortgaged houses, our retirement accounts, our health, our marriages, or the future that awaits our children, we can trust nothing, feel certain or assured about nothing. (Just 15 percent of Americans believe that today's children will be better off than their parents.)[5] For many, our lives, public and private, have come to feel like the discomfort and unease we experience the day or two before we get really sick. Our life is like a scratchy throat.

Some people, when they face this crisis or sense this malaise, may quit their job, have an affair, or medicate. (Americans lead the world in consumption of antidepressants per capita. Because of the headaches, I am patriotically doing my part.) Politically, if the 1970s provide any guide, they might hitch their wagon to a starry-eyed optimist like Ronald Reagan, or, more likely, simply check out altogether.

As for me, early one morning, I left my wife and daughter sleeping in their beds, got in my car, and drove three and a half hours to Camden, New Jersey. It rained the whole way.

I.

Camden, I admit, may not seem like the first place in America to seek a cure for your or anyone else's malaise. Camden is more like the world capital of malaise. From 2008 to 2012, the unemployment rate for Camden averaged just under 24 percent. With so few jobs, it is no wonder that two out of every five people in Camden live in poverty. Even more children—about one out of every two—live in poverty, which means that many, many more live within hailing distance of poverty.[6] Unsurprisingly, given the high rate of child poverty, the high school graduation rate in Camden suffers, but not even I could believe it is a scant 49 percent.[7]

In addition to its poverty, the city has earned its reputation as the most dangerous place in the United States. In 2008, there were more violent crimes per capita in Camden than in any other city in the country. Then, in 2011, facing budget cuts, the city laid off nearly half of its police force, and still more murders, rapes, robberies, aggravated assaults, and burglaries occurred. Now, after the layoffs, unless someone is hurt, the police no longer respond to crimes like breaking and entering or car theft, and many of the street corners in Camden have become open drug markets. The drug of choice is called "wet": marijuana soaked in liquid PCP. It causes hallucinations. In August of 2012, one woman under its influence decapitated her two-year-old son. That same month, another man high on the drug broke into a Camden house and slit the throats of a six-year-old boy and his twelve-year-old sister.[8]

All is not totally lost in Camden, of course. Driving across the Delaware River from Philadelphia on the Benjamin Franklin Bridge, you can see efforts at urban renewal. Along the refurbished waterfront, the city has invested in a baseball stadium, an aquarium, an outdoor amphitheater, and a battleship museum.

But this is a facade. To understand Camden, what matters is what used to rise along the waterfront, what the tourist traps have replaced. The most prominent sight on the city skyline is the clock tower of RCA Building #17. As its name and number suggest, the building was once surrounded by factories that used to produce records, radios, and television sets for RCA Victor. Now, RCA Building #17, the lone surviving building, rents luxury apartments. Adjacent to the RCA factory, or what used to be the RCA factory and is now an enormous parking lot, is Campbell's Field, where the Camden Riversharks play baseball. Back in the day, Campbell's—of Campbell's Soup—did more than just lease the naming rights to a baseball stadium. For decades it operated its

flagship cannery here, until it began shifting jobs from Camden in the 1950s and 1960s and finally demolished the factory in 1991. Farther down the coast, toward the Walt Whitman Bridge, lie the remains of the New York Shipbuilding Corporation, once the largest shipbuilding yards in the country. It closed in 1967. All these industries, like romantic Ireland in W. B. Yeats's "Nineteen Hundred and Nineteen," are dead and gone, and when they left, they took tens of thousands of jobs with them.[9]

Farther into the city, you can see the results of this massive experiment in deindustrialization. At first glance, the city does not seem to live up to its reputation. True, the roads are impassable in places, full of potholes and inadvertent speed bumps caused by the cycle of winter freezes and thaws and a city too broke to maintain its roads. But other than that, the downtown looks like any other burned-out industrial town. (I was born in northeastern Ohio, buckle of the Rust Belt, so I admit that these forsaken cities may disturb me less than they should.) Once you leave the waterfront and downtown, though, things quickly turn grim. Along Haddon Avenue, miles of turn-of-the-century row houses and shops line the street, most of them with boarded-up windows. Off Haddon, off pretty much any main street in Camden, in fact, many of the houses have been torn down, turning much of the city into abandoned, overgrown lots, broken up every so often by a boarded-up house or one that looks as if it is not long from that fate.

But here is all you need to know about Camden. Driving across the Benjamin Franklin Bridge from Philadelphia to Camden is free. Driving across the Benjamin Franklin Bridge from Camden to Philadelphia costs $5. Instead of making Camden a better place to live, we charge people for the privilege of leaving it.

Be that as it may, I did not come to Camden for the marijuana soaked in PCP, for the murder, for the unemployment, or even for the moral outrage, but for the same reason that many people came to Camden in the closing decades of the nineteenth century. Because that was where the poet Walt Whitman lived, and many people absolutely had to see the man in person—or, in my case, what remained of his person, his house. "Come closer to me," Whitman had written in the first line of one of his very first poems, and many, including myself, heeded the call.[10]

Whitman is why I left wife and daughter behind, why I made my pilgrimage to Camden. Because when I felt at my absolute worst, when I felt like the malaise would overwhelm me, I started reading Walt Whitman. And not to put too fine of a point on it, he saved my life. He could not do much for my headaches, alas, but reading Whitman, I did learn how to die. I learned how to accept and even celebrate our (relatively speaking) imminent death. Just as important, I learned how to live: how to have better sex, what to do about money, and, perhaps best of all, how we might survive our fetid democracy without coming away stinking ourselves.

Walt Whitman lived one hundred and fifty years ago. He never had as many readers as he wanted or felt he deserved, and in many respects, not least when it comes to his sexuality, he remains something of a mystery. Nevertheless, he is the greatest poet America ever had, and, read closely, I am convinced he is the cure for what ails us.

II.

Walt Whitman was born in 1819 in West Hills, New York, on Long Island, and moved with his family to Brooklyn when he was not quite four years old. Like many children from working-class families (his father was, at various times, a farmer, carpenter, and house builder), Whitman left school before he turned twelve. He

Walt Whitman in 1855

worked as an office boy, and at age thirteen he was apprenticed to a printer. In his late teens and early twenties, he taught school in various Long Island small towns. There he made his first tentative steps into journalism and Democratic Party politics. In 1841, he moved to New York City, and over the next few years wrote for various newspapers and published very bad short stories in literary magazines. In 1845, he left the city and moved back in with his family in Brooklyn. Shortly thereafter, Whitman became editor of the *Brooklyn Daily Eagle*. Within two years, though, he lost the job when he got ahead of the Democratic Party, which controlled the newspaper, on the issue of slavery. Whitman opposed the extension of slavery into the western territories newly acquired during the recently concluded Mexican

Walt Whitman House in Camden (1890)

War. His Party dithered on the issue. After a brief sojourn in New Orleans, in 1849 Whitman returned to Brooklyn, where he sold articles to newspapers and, like his father, took up house building.[11]

Then everything changed.

No one is quite sure how, or even when, but at some point in the first half of the 1850s, probably around 1853 or 1854, Whitman began writing some of the strangest, most ambitious, and moving poetry in all of American literature. Overnight, it seemed, he went from unenthusiastic house builder and middling journalist to inspired prophet and groundbreaking poet. In 1855, he self-published *Leaves of Grass*, which consisted of a visionary preface about the responsibility of the poet in America and twelve untitled poems that did not rhyme and did not keep a soothing, iambic beat and therefore did not seem, for some readers, like poetry at all. The first edition of the book

Thomas Eakins, Portrait of Walt Whitman, *1887*

contained Whitman's masterpiece, a long, erotic, omnivorous poem he would eventually call "Song of Myself." In the opening lines of the poem, he wrote:

> I celebrate myself,
> And what I assume you shall assume,
> For every atom belonging to me as good belongs to you.
>
> I loafe and invite my soul,
> I lean and loafe at my ease . . . . observing a spear
>   of summer grass.[12]

In a way, these lines contain all of the poetry Whitman would go on to write. Almost everything, that is, is there from the start: Whitman's sense of the divinity of all human beings (what allows him to celebrate himself); his interest in science (every atom); his

commitment to equality (the equivalence and exchangeability of
those atoms); his tendency to speak directly to his reader (you);
his urge to study what everyone takes for granted (the spear of
summer grass, in which he discovers all of life and creation). The
only thing missing, perhaps, is Whitman's intense love for the
human body. A few lines below the ones quoted above, Whitman
writes, "Welcome is every organ and attribute of me, and of any
man hearty and clean. / Not an inch nor a particle of an inch is
vile, and none shall be less familiar than the rest."[13] In a contem-
porary review, the illustrious critic Charles Eliot Norton, one of
the few people to actually read the first edition of *Leaves of Grass*,
described the poems in it, including "Song of Myself," as a "com-
pound of the New England transcendentalist and the New York
rowdy," which still seems spot on.[14]

Whitman devoted the rest of his life to *Leaves of Grass*, adding
new poems, bringing out new editions, seeking to become what
he wanted more than anything else in the world to become but
never, in his lifetime anyway, quite became: the poet whom
Americans—all Americans—read as though their lives and the
life of their country depended on it.

During the Civil War, Whitman became a volunteer nurse in
the army hospitals in Washington, D.C., and then settled into
a government clerkship in the attorney general's office. But in
1873 he had a stroke that left his left arm and leg paralyzed. A few
months later, he resigned his position in Washington and moved
in with his brother and sister-in-law, who then occupied a house
at 322 Stevens Street in Camden. (Today, 322 Stevens Street is a
vacant, unkempt lot—even the sidewalk is gone.) Later that year,
Whitman's brother moved down the street to 431 Stevens Street
(also now a vacant lot, though the sidewalk at least remains). In
1884, as his brother prepared to move from Camden to the coun-
tryside, Whitman purchased a two-story house at 328 Mickle

Street, where he lived out the remainder of his life, dying in 1892 at age seventy-two.

At the Mickle Street house, and before that at his brother's house on Stevens Street two blocks away, Whitman received a string of visitors, famous and obscure, or then famous and now obscure, who sought out the poet. Among others, these included the naturalist John Burroughs; the poet Henry Wadsworth Longfellow; the Irish novelist (of *Dracula* fame) Bram Stoker; the artist Thomas Eakins, who painted a portrait of Whitman; the writer Hamlin Garland; "three Hindus," as Whitman described them in his diary; and the journalist, diplomat, and future Librarian of Congress John Russell Young.[15] On the lecture circuit in the United States in 1882, the Irish writer Oscar Wilde came twice, once in January and again in May. "Before I leave America," Wilde wrote Whitman between visits, "I must see you again—there is no one in this wide great world of America whom I love and honour so much."[16]

Even before Whitman moved to Camden, his readers had sought him out. When Whitman published the first edition of *Leaves of Grass* in 1855, he sent a copy to the most influential writer in America, the poet and essayist Ralph Waldo Emerson. Emerson responded with a short letter full of praise. "I greet you at the beginning of a great career," he wrote. He would have written sooner, he said, but "I did not know until I last night saw the book advertised in a newspaper that I could trust the name as real and available for a post-office." Emerson closed with: "I wish to see my benefactor, and have felt much like striking my tasks and visiting New York to pay my respects."[17] Emerson, though, could not strike his tasks. (He would later look up Whitman when the poet was in Boston in 1860 overseeing publication of the third edition of *Leaves of Grass*.) In his place, Emerson sent Amos Bronson Alcott (father of Louisa May Alcott) and Henry David

Thoreau, who called on the poet at his Brooklyn home and left
impressed if somewhat mystified.

Whether to Brooklyn or, more often, to Camden, all came, all
struck their tasks, because after reading Whitman, they wanted
to pay their respects, and because, like Emerson, they could
scarcely believe that a person like Whitman could really exist.
But exist he did. There was a man, and now there is a house, if no
longer a man, to prove it.

III.

I admit I had not always felt so strongly about Whitman. Or
rather, I had felt strongly *about* him, just not strongly *for* him.
For most of my twenties, I was a fire-breathing socialist, and
Whitman, though one of the few canonical poets to come from
a working-class background, had not, I believed, been nearly
socialist enough.

Nor, I believed, had he been nearly melancholic enough.
Whitman seemed defiantly unbothered by the cruelty and stu-
pidity of the universe, especially the cruelty and stupidity of
death. Without knowing it, I shared the philosopher William
James's estimate of Whitman, who, James said, had "a tem-
perament organically weighted on the side of cheer and fatally
forbidden to linger . . . over the darker aspects of the universe."
Whitman's optimism, James believed, amounted to a kind of
"indiscriminate hurrahing for the universe" and had "become
quasi-pathological."[18] For me, a young man seeking to impress
others with his intellectual seriousness, this optimism clearly
would not do. No one is impressed by yes-men. Instead, I looked
to those who, as Herman Melville said of Nathaniel Hawthorne,
said "NO! in thunder," and who "the Devil himself cannot make

Whitman in his Camden bedroom—note the mess.

say *yes*."[19] That is, I took my cues about the futility of love from the likes of T. S. Eliot's "The Love Song of J. Alfred Prufrock" and my conclusions about the finality of death from poems like *The Waste Land.* Next to these hard-boiled writers, Whitman seemed downright soft.

Nor did I always believe that Whitman would save America from what ailed it. More often than not I thought he was—or represented—exactly what it suffered from. His naive optimism, his boosterish patriotism, his fuzzy spiritualism, his celebration of the body and sex—though these may have once seemed, in the nineteenth century perhaps, like the solution to a problem, they now seemed like the problem itself. Americans did not need to be told to look on the bright side, to love America, to trust God, or, my Lord, to worship sex. They needed to be told not to.

But I know now that I was wrong. At some point, and for me it came in my early thirties, you realize that socialism will be a long time coming in the United States, especially when one of our two political parties fervently believes that the United States is already on the road to socialist serfdom. When you wake up to this reality, you care a lot less about whether a poet was socialist enough or not, and a lot more about how he can help you live in the world you have.

I was less wrong to resent Whitman's pathological optimism, but wrong nonetheless and in ways that really mattered. Whitman did write that "what is called good is perfect and what is called bad is just as perfect," which William James thought was plain silly.[20] But Whitman's optimism, as James believed, was not "congenital." Or not merely congenital. Whitman may have been born that way, but he had reasons for his optimism, and for his "indiscriminate hurrahing for the universe." And when you look into those reasons, as I had never really done before, the hurrahing does not seem nearly so indiscriminate—or not so pathological, anyway. Indeed, it may be less pathology than cure.

As you might gather from the title and subtitle of this book, I have changed my mind about Whitman and his place in America, too. True, when it comes to the country of reality, many Americans, as prosecutors say, are a flight risk. Too many elements of our culture, especially our popular and political culture, teach us, as the polemicist Chris Hedges puts it, that "we can be whoever we seek to be, that we live in the greatest country on earth, that we are endowed with superior moral and physical qualities, and that our future will always be glorious and prosperous, either because of our own attributes or our national character or because we are blessed by God."[21] At times, Whitman can seem to join the chorus of voices indulging and even encouraging

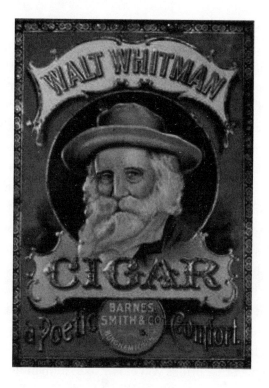

The Walt Whitman cigar

Americans in these beliefs. As a people, we occasionally celebrate ourselves altogether too much.

But Whitman had nothing to do with building up the empire of illusions that currently enfold and enthrall Americans, not just because few people actually read him, then or now, and therefore you cannot lay much blame at his door. But also because—read carefully—he says no such things. Indeed, I am now convinced that reading Whitman would go far toward striking back against that empire of illusion.

IV.

I arrived at Whitman's small, two-story frame house at ten in the morning on a June day convulsed by thunderstorms. In Whitman's time, Camden was an up-and-coming industrial city, and Mickle Street was a bustling residential block. Today the three adjacent houses owned by the state of New Jersey, including Whitman's, are some of the last houses standing on the block. Across the street from the Whitman house, you face the walled-off backs of the Brutalist-style Camden County Jail and the Camden Courthouse, both of which seemed to account for what traffic came and went on the street that morning. Other than that, there is not much to look at.

The Whitman house is lovingly maintained. It looks much like what it would have looked like when Whitman lived there. It has period furniture and many of Whitman's own personal effects, including his favorite rocking chair, the bed he died in, and, the object that brings you closer to Whitman than anything else, a pair of his shoes. Black. Size 11. (At just a hair under six feet, Whitman was tall for his time.) The shoes are tucked under another rocking chair in his upstairs bedroom, where Whitman did most of his writing. The curators of the house have gestured toward the avalanche of papers that once spread across his bedroom floor—when he died, his friends removed paper by the barrelful—but reproducing it exactly would leave little room for visitors like me to walk and probably be a fire hazard. In any event, it is easy enough to imagine Whitman seated at his table in front of the window that faced Mickle Street, dashing off poems while his pet canary sang in its cage.

For all of that, I should admit that trips to the preserved houses of famous poets always leave me vaguely disappointed, and Whitman's house was no exception. We love poets for what they say, not where or how they lived. We admire them for what makes them different from us, their poetry, and not what makes them like us, the fact that they lived in a home or sat in a chair or wore shoes. I have a house. I have a bed. I wear shoes. I did not, however, write "Song of Myself." Time spent at a poet's house, where he once lived, always feels like the time could be better spent just reading the poetry, where he now lives on.

Equally disappointing is the gift shop or, rather, the lack of one. The website mentions one, but I was told it is still a work in progress. That is too bad, because I desperately wanted a Walt Whitman mug or T-shirt, and I would not have said no to a plush doll Whitman for my three-year-old daughter. I thought Whitman would look comical among her menagerie of stuffed lions, lambs, tigers, and panda bears. ("I think I could turn and live awhile with the animals / They are so placid and self-contained," Whitman wrote in "Song of Myself.")[22] I had to settle for buying something off the Internet, which, happily, turned out not to require settling at all. In addition to pornography, the Internet, it seems, was invented to sell custom gifts. As a result, you can find Whitman's picture and words on mugs and T-shirts, but also on throw pillows, area rugs, blankets, aprons, coasters, pet bowls, magnets, buttons, golf balls, bumper stickers, toiletry bags, beer can coolers, shot glasses, flasks, wall clocks, bracelets, iPhone cases, even thongs. There is nothing, apparently, that an image of Whitman or a cloying quotation from him cannot adorn.

A purist might object to such commercialism, viewing it as the triumph of image over text and thus a further sign of our illiteracy. Or, perhaps even worse, they might view it as no more than personal branding: admire me because I admire Walt Whitman.

But Whitman took a different view. By the time of his last years in Camden, as he grew slightly more famous, Whitman was already

becoming a brand. In 1890, his friend and biographer Horace
Traubel visited the poet at his Camden house—as he did almost
every day—and brought with him a cigar label from a Binghamton,
New York company that was retailing a Walt Whitman cigar.
Surprisingly, Whitman approved of it. "Had with me likewise a
copy of 'Walt Whitman cigar' envelope (Binghamton: Ostrom,
Barnes & Co.)," Traubel wrote in his nine-volume record of his
conversations with the poet, *With Walt Whitman in Camden*.
"Laughed much over it—W[hitman] thinking, 'That is fame!'
And again, 'It is not so bad—not as bad as it might be: give the hat
a little more height and it would not be such an offense.'" [23]

As his response suggests, Whitman did not object to fame.
More often than not, he seems to have craved it. Not for its own
sake, I think, but because he approved of anything—including
cigar labels and probably thongs—that might lead people to his
poetry, that might generate readers, which is all he really wanted.
"The proof of a poet," Whitman concluded his "Preface" to the
1855 edition of *Leaves of Grass*, "is that his country absorbs
him as affectionately as he has absorbed it." [24] If a Whitman cigar
helped American readers absorb Whitman, so be it. For seem-
ingly no other reason than to attract those readers, he put a rous-
ing sea battle in the middle of "Song of Myself."

Like Whitman, I want America to absorb him, and so I con-
ceived this book as a sort of Whitman cigar box, as an advertise-
ment for the man but even more so for his poetry. I hope that
it brings Whitman new readers, or reminds old readers of what
they can find in his poetry. When I felt my lowest, when daily life
weighed me down, when I despaired of my country and myself,
he lifted me up. And I believe he can do the same for others and
for the country as a whole. Whitman, as I say, saved my life. This
is a book about how Walt Whitman can save America's life, too.

Each chapter identifies a source for our contemporary

malaise, whether it is death, money, sex, or democracy, and then looks to a particular Whitman poem for relief from it. I spend some time with the poems, trying to make plain what, exactly, Whitman wrote and what he believed. But I also try to bring the poems to life. I show how they emerged from Whitman's life and times, and I re-create the places and incidents (crossing the East River, visiting wounded soldiers in army hospitals) that inspired Whitman to write the poems. The result is a mix of biography, literary criticism, manifesto, and, I am not embarrassed to say, self-help. God knows, we need it.

That, by the way, is why I like the Walt Whitman cigar label so much. The picture of Whitman, as he himself joked, was not so bad, even if the hat could be taller. Even better, though, is the slogan: "A Poetic Comfort." It means (I think) that a Walt Whitman cigar comforts in much the same way that poetry and, in particular, the poetry of Walt Whitman, comforts. In this book, I skip the cigar and go right to the source. In a time of personal, philosophical, and political affliction, I have found Whitman "A Poetic Comfort," and I believe others will as well.

In the closing lines of "Song of Myself," Whitman, staging his own death and taking his leave of the reader, writes:

I bequeath myself to the dirt to grow from the grass I love,
If you want me again look for me under your boot-soles.

You will hardly know who I am or what I mean,
But I shall be good health to you nevertheless,[25]

In this book, I try to explain who Whitman was and what he means because, unlike a Whitman cigar, Whitman the poet can be good health to us indeed, especially now, in the moment of our very real malaise, when many of us need it most.

CHAPTER 1

Congratulations! You're Dead!

Lovers of me, bafflers of graves.
—WALT WHITMAN, "Song of Myself" (1855)

I n the first centuries of the Roman Empire, you took your chances being a Christian. Occasionally, some far-flung Roman prefect would rouse himself long enough to bully you or one of your brethren, which could mean anything from exile to, more grandiosely, an appointment with the lions.

In the early years of the third century, a Christian theologian, Tertullian, sought to win religious tolerance from the Roman Empire for his persecuted fellow Christians. In *Apologeticus*, Tertullian explains that though Christians respected the emperor—at the time, the unusually brutal Septimius Severus—they could not worship him since he was no god, let alone *the* God. Tertullian then offered some legalistic reasoning about why this should not bother any right-thinking emperor, why, in fact, an emperor should prefer to be thought of as a man and not a god. Only men, Tertullian observes, could be emperors. "To call him god," Tertullian suggests, somewhat snidely, "is to rob him of his title. If he is not a man, emperor he cannot be." Tertullian implies that this argument should not come as news to an emperor; he knows in his heart that he is a man and not a god. Tertullian

East River ferryboat

writes: "Even when, amid the honors of a triumph, he sits on that lofty chair, he is reminded that he is only human. A voice at his back keeps whispering in his ear, 'Look behind thee. Remember thou art but a man.'"[1]

Tertullian's description of the emperor's "voice at his back" may be the source for the belief that during "triumphs," the lavish ceremonies held to celebrate Roman military victories, a slave would follow behind the returned conquering emperor and whisper in his ear, "*Respice te, hominem te memento*": Remember, you are only a man. Or, more simply, the slave is supposed to have whispered, "*Memento mori*": Remember, you die.[2]

In all likelihood, there was no whispering slave. The evidence for it beyond Tertullian's account is slim, and Tertullian seems to be describing what an emperor must be thinking to himself, not what someone is actually whispering to him. But the image makes an impression nonetheless. Here is no inert skull, the usual reminder of death that later Christians (and Christian painters) would favor, but a living, breathing *memento mori*. Someone

For Christians, a *memento mori* does not just remind you of your mortality but, rather, of which world—this one or the next—you should hold dear. The Ash Wednesday invocation, "Ashes to ashes, dust to dust," and the command that usually follows, "Turn away from sin and be faithful to the Gospel," offer a similar reminder. Forget your body, which dies, and forget the earth, through which you're merely passing. Rather, focus on your soul, which lives on, in heaven or hell, depending on whether you turn toward or away from God.

Like a lot of people, I do not believe in a soul distinct from a body, nor in heaven or hell, and I think this world, this life, is the only one we have. So when I think about death, I am reminded that, sad to say, this body, this world, is it. For some, that thought might lead them to follow other Latin maxims, whether *carpe diem* or, as Horace put it, *nunc est bibendum* (now is the time to drink). For me, the thought of my own death just leads to simmering despair and, quite frankly, nauseating fear. I confess that my imagination can get carried away. On my deathbed, I wonder, what will be the last thought that passes through my mind? Whose face will be the last one that flashes on my consciousness? What will I regret? And then what? The "total emptiness forever," as another poet, Philip Larkin, put it.

> . . . no sight, no sound,
> No touch or taste or smell, nothing to think with,
> Nothing to love or link with,
> The anaesthetic from which none come round.[3]

Because of these appalling prospects, though I might often think of my death, at the same time I tend not to linger over it for very long. It is simply too horrifying to contemplate. When you die, you will no longer *be*. The light will go out, and the whose job it is to remind you that, at the height of your triumph, you die.

Triumphant emperors may have needed such a reminder. I do not. Indeed, a slave would be wasting his breath on me, because I think about death, including my own, daily, even more so as I cross the midway of my life's journey, as Dante put it, and even more so since my wife and I had a daughter a few years ago. As with household chores, my wife and I share the burden of worrying about death. I worry about what would happen if I die; she worries about what would happen if she dies; we each worry about what would happen if the other dies, or what would happen to our daughter if we both die; and, though this is harder to fathom, we try to imagine what would happen (as recently happened to two different acquaintances of ours) if our child should die. In short, we need no one to remind us that we die. We are doing just fine on our own.

Unlike Tertullian, though, we are not Christians. I am not anything, in fact, except an ordinary atheist. As a result, I remember that I die to slightly different effect than do most Christians.

View of Brooklyn from the foot of Wall Street, 1855

darkness will overwhelm you. Everything shall become nothing. The total emptiness forever. It seems so terribly cruel: to be given life only to have every last speck of it taken away.

Who wants that drink now?

Walt Whitman is remembered as a poet of many things: the city, democracy, the human body, sex, even the Civil War. Few remember him as a poet of death. That is a mistake. In many ways, death is his great theme, though he treats it unlike any poet then or since.

That was why I found myself, one overcast June morning, aboard the East River Ferry. The East River, with its view of Manhattan to the west and Brooklyn to the east, provided Whitman with the scene for his great poem about transcendence and immortality, "Crossing Brooklyn Ferry." I dragged myself to Brooklyn and boarded the ferry because I wanted to live where Whitman lived, see what Whitman saw, and feel what he felt—or what remained of it. Not just because I wanted to know Whitman better, or bask in the aura, though there is something to that, but because in "Crossing Brooklyn Ferry" Whitman suggests that if you could see what he sees and experience what he experiences, these shared visions and experiences would reveal the hidden scheme of the universe. More important still, he promises that they would reveal how each of us, both our living and our dying, fits into that scheme. "To die is different than anyone supposed, and luckier," Whitman writes in "Song of Myself," from 1855, and "Crossing Brooklyn Ferry," from 1856, comes about as close as Whitman ever comes to showing why death is different—and luckier—than everyone supposes.[4] And though I cannot, finally, accept Whitman's comforting thoughts about death, his other reflections on the nature of the universe, especially its indifference to property, can make us feel better—less fearful and, possibly, less angry—about dying.

I.

In the 1850s, the ferry from Brooklyn to Manhattan across the East River meant almost everything to Whitman. An aficionado of opera, the theater, and the chaotic city life of Manhattan, Whitman in the afternoons often left Brooklyn, where he then lived, and traveled by the Fulton Ferry across the East River to Manhattan. In later years, he would recall his "passion for ferries." "My life," he noted of this time, "was curiously identified with Fulton Ferry, already becoming the greatest of its sort in the world for general importance, volume, variety, rapidity, and picturesqueness." He recalled that "almost daily, I cross'd on the boats." On board, Whitman befriended the boat pilots. "The Balsirs, Johnny Cole, Ira Smith, William White, and my young ferry friend, Tom Gere—how well I remember them well," he wrote in 1882.[5]

In 1883, however, not long after Whitman fondly recalled his friends the boat pilots, the Fulton Ferry was being made all but obsolete by the opening of the Brooklyn Bridge. Symbolically, the bridge towered above the Fulton Street landing in Brooklyn. Increasingly anachronistic, the ferry would stop service altogether in 1924. In June 2011, just in time for me to retrace Whitman's journey, New York Waterway, a private company, partnered with the city to restart ferry service across the East River, and riders today take the exact route Whitman did in the 1850s.[6]

The ferry may travel the same route Whitman did in the 1850s, but it surveys a far different scene. In "Crossing Brooklyn Ferry," Whitman lovingly catalogues the visions that dazzled him as he chugged across the East River. "I too many and many a time crossed the river of old," Whitman writes, and

Look'd toward the lower bay to notice the vessels arriving,
Saw their approach, saw aboard those that were near me,
Saw the white sails of schooners and sloops, saw the ships
    at anchor,
The sailors at work in the rigging or astride the spars,
The round masts, the swinging motion of the hulls,
    the slender serpentine pennants,
The large and small steamers in motion, the pilots in their
    pilot-houses,
The white wake left by the passage, the quick tremulous
    whirl of the wheels,
The flags of all nations, the falling of them at sunset,
The scallop-edged waves in the twilight, the ladled cups,
    the frolicsome crests and glistening,
The stretch afar growing dimmer and dimmer, the gray
    walls of the granite storehouses by the docks,
On the river the shadowy group, the big steam-tug closely
    flank'd on each side by the barges, the hay-boat,
    the belated lighter,
On the neighboring shore, the fires from the foundry chimneys
    burning high and glaringly into the night,
Casting their flicker of black contrasted with wild red and
    yellow light over the roof tops of houses, and down
    into the clefts of the street.[7]

Today, by contrast, you see far less. Most of the ships are gone, and the sailors, too. From the deck of the ferry, if you look toward the lower bay, as Whitman did, to the south and southwest, down the Brooklyn coastline, you see cars along the Brooklyn-Queens Expressway and the barren docks and the spires of cranes of the Red Hook Container Terminal. In the bay itself, perhaps the most notable sight is the ventilation building on Governor's

Island that serves the Brooklyn–Battery tunnel. Way off on the horizon, peaking behind the skyscrapers of the financial district, is the Statue of Liberty, dedicated in 1886, long after Whitman had left the city.

Truth be told, the view does not inspire. I am not sure even Whitman could make poetry out of the BQE. And the Container Terminal looks like the parking lot for a superstore no one frequents. If I were less concerned about offending Whitman, I would call the whole vista ugly.

Even so, you can see enough to glimpse what Whitman saw. The gray walls of the granite storehouses are still there, the docks are still there (sort of), and you can still make out the rooftops of houses and the clefts of streets. Most important of all, though, the river is still there.

Why does what you see from the East River Ferry matter? Because, Whitman believes, what you see confirms your immortality. Unlikely as it may seem, Whitman suggests, in these things—buildings, docks, river, even the BQE—you can see why you will live forever. For Whitman, they testify to the provident design of the universe, and they make plain that death is not death but rather a form of rebirth. "It avails not," Whitman asserts early in "Crossing Brooklyn Ferry," "neither time or place—distance avails not."[8] Similarly, Whitman implies, death, which separates us from time and distances us from everyone and everything else, also avails not. In other poems written just before "Crossing Brooklyn Ferry," Whitman develops his reasoning about why this is so, but for him, his journey across the East River confirms the intuitions he outlines elsewhere. Death avails not. It is of no use. It does not accomplish the end we think it does. In effect, we outlive it, and the Brooklyn ferry proves it.

II.

"Crossing Brooklyn Ferry" begins with Whitman aboard the ferry, addressing—commanding—the flood tide of the river to "flow on!" He then claims to watch the flood tide "face to face," so too the clouds of the west and the setting sun, which he also sees "face to face." In the lines that follow, Whitman stops addressing the natural world and starts addressing "you"—that is, us, his reader. He states that he finds the crowds of men and women aboard the ferryboats more curious than we might suppose. But Whitman does not stop with the crowds of people he can see. He also claims that "you that shall cross from shore to shore years hence" are also more to him, and more in his thoughts, than we might suppose.[9] The direct address is startling. I am thinking of you, reader, Whitman says, and no one else, and for a moment you cannot help but believe him.

Whitman then pauses to reflect on his place in the universe. Things, Whitman implies, give him life. "The impalpable sustenance of me from all things at all hours of the day," he writes. Moreover, he concludes that he is part of a "simple, compact, well-joined scheme."[10] (Here one can see Whitman the carpenter: "well-joined" refers to joinery, the craft of joining two pieces of wood not with nails but through matching cuts in the wood, like a rabbet and dado.) At this point, Whitman does not reveal the nature of this scheme, and he is only slightly more revealing later in the poem, but he does insist that though he and others may appear to be discrete individuals, they in fact belong to the same scheme. How does he know? Because he can see the "ties" between himself and those who will follow him.[11] Others, he observes, just as I did that June morning, will enter the gates of the ferry and cross from shore to shore, and, in so doing, they will see the same things the poet saw: the run of the flood tide, the ships of Manhattan to the north and west, the heights of Brooklyn to the south and east, the islands large and small, and the setting sun.

For Whitman, these shared visions allow those who see them to transcend time, place, and distance. Aboard the East River Ferry, I see more or less what Whitman saw. He and I share a connection. But Whitman and I—or you, or anyone who sees what he sees—share more than just a connection. Whitman seems to imply that we share a common existence. "Just as you feel when you look on the river and sky, so I felt," Whitman writes,

> Just as any of you is one of a living crowd, I was one of a crowd,
> Just as you are refresh'd by the gladness of the river, and the
>   bright flow, I was refresh'd,
> Just as you stand and lean on the rail, yet hurry with the swift
>   current, I stood, and yet was hurried,
> Just as you look on the numberless masts of ships, and the
>   thick stemm'd pipes of steamboats, I look'd.[12]

If, as Whitman earlier claims, we are influenced by—perhaps even derived from—the things around us, then when others witness or experience those same things, they will in some important way become like us, perhaps even become us. In short, you are what you see.

If so, then even though I die, Whitman says, I will be near to you because you now look at what I looked at. We are looking at the same things, and those things unite us. We share a vision, and thus we share an identity. At that moment, I am you and you are me.

What follows is the passage quoted above, the one in which Whitman describes what he sees as he looks toward Brooklyn and the lower bay, further connecting us to him through these closely observed visions. But as the poem progresses, Whitman insists that more unites us than just what we see. Places and objects unite us, yes, but so too do more intangible things, like questions about the universe, which, the poet claims, he also felt stir within him, and which also came upon him in his walks home late at night or as he lay in his bed. Our bodies also unite us—not that we share bodies but that we each have one, and therefore share the experience of having a body.

More significantly, what Whitman calls "the dark patches" also unite us. In one of the most powerful passages in the poem, Whitman writes:

It is not upon you alone the dark patches fall,
The dark threw patches down upon me also,
The best I had done seemed to me blank and suspicious,
My great thoughts, as I supposed them, were they not
in reality meagre? Would not people laugh at me?

It is not you alone who know what it is to be evil,
I am he who knew what it was to be evil,
I too knitted the old knot of contrariety,
Blabbed, blushed, resented, lied, stole, grudged,
Had guile, anger, lust, hot wishes I dared not speak,
Was wayward, vain, greedy, shallow, sly, a solitary committer,
a coward, a malignant person,
The wolf, the snake, the hog, not wanting in me,
The cheating look, the frivolous word, the adulterous wish,
not wanting,
Refusals, hates, postponements, meanness, laziness, none
of these wanting.[13]

Whitman balances these dark patches and evil instances with a recitation of other, less dispiriting experiences. I was also free, friendly, and proud, he says. I was on a first-name basis with many people around the city. Like us, too, or so he imagines, Whitman regrets that he never tells these people whom he called by their first names that he loved them. Yet he also recognizes that, like others, more often than not his days are not tragic but ordinary. I lived the same life as everyone else, he says, the same old laughing, gnawing, sleeping, and, like others, played a minor part on the stage of history.

Following these lines, Whitman ventures—and I believe he is right—that he has gained our confidence. "Closer yet I approach you," he boasts, certain that since he has confessed his doubts and errors, and certain that since you have no doubt harbored those same doubts and errors, that you and he have now formed an even tighter bond.[14]

He then says something that, at first glance, appears paradoxical: "I considered long and seriously of you before you were born." Of course, this statement cannot be literally true. Whitman cannot have considered long and seriously of me before I was born because there was no "me" for him to consider of. What he seems to mean, instead, is that he considered long and seriously of what I must be—that is, me to the extent that I share qualities or characteristics with himself and others. In other words, Whitman means I considered long and seriously of human beings, and since you are a human being, I considered long and seriously of you. Again, Whitman bypasses what individualizes us for what unites us.

The poem grows even spookier when in the lines that follow Whitman suggests that he lives on, that he may even be enjoying this, by which he means, presumably, us reading of how he considered long and seriously of us before we were born. "Who knows," he asks, "but I am as good as looking at you now, for all you cannot see me?"[15] Yes, Whitman is claiming to watch you as you read him. Frustratingly, he does not give us a reason why he thinks this, but only raises it as a possibility. Equally frustrating, he hints that he knows more than he is letting on. "Every thing indicates," he writes, but he does not say what it indicates, only that everything, including our souls, is shrouded in "a necessary film," which suggests that whatever it is that everything indicates, it may be hard to see.[16]

Nevertheless, Whitman, like an impatient philosopher, states that it is all perfectly clear. "We understand each other, then, do we not?" he writes, and jauntily plows ahead:

> What I promised without mentioning it, have you
>   not accepted?
> What the study could not teach—what the preaching could not
>   accomplish is accomplished, is it not?
> What the push of reading could not start is started by me
>   personally, is it not?[17]

Alas, Whitman does this sort of thing all the time. He does not argue or convince; he assumes, and then moves on, in his mind, to the more interesting business of describing, illustrating, and sometimes taunting those who do not share his assumptions.

At times, this method can leave you wondering what in the world Whitman is on about. In "Crossing Brooklyn Ferry," the clue, I think, lies in his phrase "what the preaching could not accomplish." To preach means, of course, to speak in public on religious matters. Another, more specific sense is to preach the gospel, and the gospel, as your friend who studied Latin can tell you, means the good news, the good story (*god* equals good and *spel* equals story). Later, people will take *god* (good) to mean

God, and thus "good news" and "good story" to mean "God news," "God story." In other words, Whitman is telling us the good news, the news about God. However, he is merely telling us that there is good news—not what the news is. He gives us the headline without the story.

Unfortunately, at this point, we are more or less at the end of the poem. Whitman revisits all the things he has seen and described in the poem: the river, the flood tide, the ebb tide, the waves, the clouds, the crowds of passengers, the tall masts of ships, the beautiful hills of Brooklyn, the seagulls, and so on, and urges each thing to do what it does. Whitman implies that if we have any lingering questions or doubts, these natural facts will answer them, but it feels like someone is repeating an explanation you do not understand only this time more loudly. The volume, or, in this case, the added poetic touches, do not clarify things. Nor do the concluding lines of the poem. Whitman continues to give orders before stopping to draw his conclusion:

> Expand, being than which none else is perhaps
>   more spiritual!
> Keep your places, objects than which none is more lasting.
> . . . .
> You have waited, you always wait, you dumb beautiful
>   ministers! you novices!
> We receive you with free sense at last, and are insatiate
>   henceforward,
> Not you any more shall be able to foil us, or withhold
>   yourselves from us,
> We use you, and do not cast you aside—we plant you
>   permanently within us,
> We fathom you not—we love you—there is perfection in
>   you also,

You furnish your parts toward eternity,
Great or small, you furnish your parts toward the soul.[18]

Although much remains ambiguous here, one thing is clear. Unlike most religions, which see this world and this life as finite and merely prelude to the next, Whitman makes no such distinctions. Instead of diminishing this world, the objects and experiences all around us, which he calls "being," he orders it to expand, since nothing else is more lasting and spiritual. Similarly, whereas in most religions the soul is something distinct from ordinary matter, for Whitman our soul derives from the objects in this world. As in the opening and closing lines of the poem, they furnish their parts toward the soul.

On the surface, the poem celebrates New York City, and Whitman comes off as the loyal native son. This place, these objects, these people made me, just as they made others before me and will go on making others after me. They furnish their parts "toward the soul," and since they will always furnish their parts toward the soul, they furnish their parts toward eternity. If so, then the least we can do is notice them. Although, what we ought to do is love them as we love ourselves and others.

At the same time, Whitman gives the impression that these objects do more than just remind us of the glories of this world. As much as we receive them with "free sense," as much as we plant them permanently within us, we do not fathom them, he writes. They have unexplored depths. At the same time, they are—in a wonderful phrase—"dumb, beautiful ministers": dumb in the sense that they do not speak, beautiful in that they are glorious, and ministers in that they, like Christian or government ministers, are the agents of some higher power. (In the original Latin, *minister* is an attendant, a servant.) "Novices," the other word Whitman uses to describe these objects, also fits with this meaning. These objects are novices not in the sense of a person new to an activity, a beginner, but in the religious sense of a new convert, a neophyte, a prospective member of a religious order.

But for what religion are these objects ministering? What higher power do they serve? To what God have they converted? Whitman does not say, but in other poems, and in parts of "Crossing Brooklyn Ferry," Whitman offers enough clues to explain what higher power these dumb, beautiful ministers serve. As we have seen early on in "Crossing Brooklyn Ferry," everyone belongs to "the simple, compact, well-joined scheme," which implies not only that there is a scheme, and that it is carefully made, but that there may be a careful maker behind it all, the ultimate joiner, as it were. It is a wonderful image given that the purpose of the poem is to overcome the isolation of our finite lives and join Whitman to everyone who comes before and after him. To understand this scheme, and its schemer, however, we need to pay closer attention to what Whitman believed about the origin and structure of the universe. Although he never comes right out with it, throughout "Crossing Brooklyn Ferry" and other poems he makes it plain enough.

III.

A few years ago I built a brick storage bench in our backyard. I dug the foundation, spread gravel, poured concrete, and began to lay bricks. As any bricklayer will tell you, the key is to keep things on the level, horizontally and vertically. Over time, master bricklayers learn to eyeball a structure and see whether it is level. The rest of us have to rely on a spirit level, those long pieces of wood, metal, or plastic with a small clear tube and a bubble inside. (Spirit levels get their name not for any ghostly reasons but because the liquid in the bubble is usually a mineral spirit like alcohol or ether.) If you are keeping your brickwork level, the bubble comes to rest between the two lines. If, like me, you are not, the bubble wanders to one side of the tube or the other.

If you have ever tried to submerge a beach ball in a swimming pool only to have it burst to the surface, you already know how spirit levels work. The short answer is gravity. (The long answer is gravity plus buoyancy.) The incredible mass of Earth creates its own gravitational pull, drawing objects close to it. If you jump in the air, for instance, you do not go floating off into space but are quickly pulled back to the ground. The force of gravity can also accumulate. For example, when I hold my daughter on my shoulders, I have to lift her up—overcome the force of gravity pressing her back toward the earth. If my wife put our daughter on her shoulders and I then tried to put both of them on my shoulders, I would have to assume the weight—the downward force of gravity—of both my wife and daughter.

The same goes for any object on the bottom of the gravitational pile. For example, water at the bottom of a drinking glass bears all the weight of the water above it. We say that the pressure is greater the deeper you go. And the difference in pressure from bottom to top tends to exert an upward force. We call this buoyancy. If you put something heavy into the glass—say a coin—gravity will pull it downward. That is, gravity exerts a stronger downward force on the coin than the buoyant pressure upward can overcome. Conversely, if you put something light into the glass, like a toothpick or an air bubble, it will rise to the surface, where the pressure is lighter. For the same reason, a beach ball filled with air rushes to the surface despite your efforts to hold it underwater.

The very same principles apply to a spirit level. The air bubble always rises to the surface of the heavier condensed liquid. The final piece of the puzzle is that the little glass tube that houses the bubble only looks straight; in fact, it curves down at the ends, like a frown or a banana. Therefore, if the surface you are measuring is level, the bubble will rise to the exact center, the highest point, and nestle pleasingly between the two lines. If the surface is at all slanted, however, the air bubble will gravitate—literally—to the highest point, but the highest point will no longer fall in the middle of the two lines. It will drift to the right or left. All thanks to gravity—and buoyancy. But mostly gravity.

Gravity does not exist just here on earth. It exerts its force everywhere in the universe. Indeed, the universe could not exist without it. Gravity caused disparate matter to coalesce into suns, planets, and moons; it set the earth spinning; and it keeps planets circulating around suns, and moons circulating around planets. Like an invisible spider's web, it holds the universe together.[19]

As an ambitious autodidact, Whitman went out of his way to learn about gravity. As a builder of houses he had firsthand experience with it. "The power by which the carpenter plumbs his house," Whitman wrote in one of his early notebooks, "is the same power that dashed his brains out if he fall from the roof."[20] ("Plumb" refers to the other way carpenters used gravity to build, this time vertically. A "plumb bob" is a weight on the end of a string that is suspended from some higher point. Because gravity pushes down on the weight, if you follow the plumb line as you build up, you will build a perfect vertical.) In his poems, too, Whitman often refers to gravity. In "Song of Myself," he writes that "I reckon I behave no prouder than the level I plant my house by after all."[21] Elsewhere in that poem, he describes himself as "Plumb in the uprights, well entretied, braced in the beams."[22] ("Entretied," by the way, simply means plastered.) In these references to the level and plumb, Whitman is talking about himself, of course, but also what allows him to be so certain of himself. As with gravity, he merely follows the laws of the universe. "I see that the elementary laws never apologize," Whitman writes in "Song of Myself," and neither shall Whitman.[23] Indeed, he occasionally speaks of gravity and these elementary laws in the same breath. In an 1855 poem, later given the title "A Song for Occupations," Whitman writes of "the attraction of gravity and the great laws and the harmonious combinations and the fluids of the air."[24] (Keep an eye on that phrase, "the fluids of the air." It will matter in a moment.)

Gravity, as these passages suggest, meant more to Whitman than just a way to keep houses standing. For Whitman, the existence of such a crucial, unerring law implied that the universe made sense. It followed a deliberate plan; it formed a "simple, compact, well-join'd scheme," as he put it in "Crossing Brooklyn Ferry." If so, then there must have been a planner, a schemer. At the least, there was a plan, a scheme, and Whitman, as others do, found this very comforting.

Admittedly, talk of plans and planners might sound like so much twaddle about intelligent design. But consider how many things, including gravity, had to go right for life to exist in the universe, indeed, for the universe even to exist. And it is not just the presence or absence of something like gravity. Gravity has to be perfect, exactly what it is, no more, no less, for the universe and for life on earth to appear. If gravity had been stronger or weaker by one infinitesimal part, for example, the sun would not exist. It would collapse in upon itself or never have formed in the first place. And the same goes for a number of other forces that shape the universe. If the electrical forces that hold atoms together were minimally stronger or weaker, they would not have converted so readily into the elements needed to create, well, all the elements (carbon, oxygen) of life. "Almost everything about the basic structure of the universe," the philosopher Robin Collins concludes, "is balanced on a razor's edge for life to occur."[25] You could call it luck, but it also looks like design or the residue of design, which would suggest the existence of some designer somewhere. In order to avoid just this conclusion, physicists speculate that many universes must exist or must have existed. In other words, the odds against suns, planets, and life occurring in any given universe are so incredible that, like monkeys at a typewriter trying to pound out *Hamlet*, you would need a million (or more) chances to produce the forces necessary to create and sustain things like suns, planets, elements, atoms, and, ultimately, life. And when you think of it that way, the existence of one universe, made by one Creator, seems comparatively plausible.[26]

Not everyone assents to these teleological arguments for God's existence. Still, they appealed to Whitman, and he was not alone. Whitman lived in an era when science did not stand opposed to religion but rather was thought to reveal the lines by which God, or some such force, laid out the universe. "It is no little matter," Whitman writes in an 1855 poem, "this round and delicious globe, moving so exactly in its orbit forever and ever, without one jolt or the untruth of a single second."[27] And it was no little matter because such orbits implied a meticulously planned universe. In the aptly titled "Faith Poem," from 1856, Whitman writes: "I do not doubt that the orbs, and the systems of orbs, play their swift sports through the air on purpose."[28] In "Song of Myself" he asks, "Did you think the celestial laws are yet to be worked over and rectified?" He leaves the question unanswered since he cannot imagine anyone answering no.[29]

Time and again, Whitman speaks of the universe and its laws, its purposes, including, for him, death, which was as much a part of the benevolent plan of the universe as gravity. In particular, Whitman seems to have drawn from his reading in astronomy and chemistry the principle of the conservation of matter, which holds that matter can neither be created nor destroyed. For Whitman, the same principle applied to life. What looked like death was merely transformation, a new birth. His favorite metaphor for this rebirth is compost. The dead are buried in the ground, and new life rises out of them. "What chemistry!" he exclaims in an 1856 poem dedicated to this theme, originally titled "Poem of Wonder at the Resurrection of the Wheat" and later simply "This Compost."[30] "The summer growth is innocent and disdainful above all those strata of sour dead," he writes.[31] Later in the poem, he expresses his terrified admiration for the earth. "It gives such divine materials to men and accepts such leavings from them at last."[32] In "Song of Myself," he writes, "As to you Corpse, I think you are good manure."[33]

Indeed, the principle of the conservation of matter provided Whitman with one of the most famous passages in all of his poetry. "A child said, What is the grass, fetching it to me with full hands," Whitman writes in "Song of Myself." After trying out a few answers, he responds:

And now it seems to me the beautiful uncut hair of graves.

Tenderly will I use you curling grass,
It may be you transpire from the breasts of young men,
It may be if I had known them I would have loved them;
It may be you are from old people and from women, and from
    offspring taken soon out of their mothers' laps,
And here you are the mothers' laps.[34]

"The smallest sprout," he continues, "shows there is no death."[35] Indeed, it made no more sense to speak of the "death" of the molecules that form your body as you pass from your bodily state to some other state (grass, some other life-form) as it did to speak of the "death" of an oxygen molecule as it combines with two hydrogen molecules to form water. In both cases, something simply becomes something else. In our universe, nothing dies. So too for the something that is us. When we die, so to speak, our souls, like our bodies, assume another form. As for molecules, so for us. "We," our essential selves, live on. In an 1856 poem, "Clef Poem," Whitman writes:

> I do not know what follows the death of my body
> But I know well that whatever it is, it is best for me.
> And I know well that what is really Me shall live just
>   as much as before.[36]

If so, then death does not mark the end of life but the beginning of a new life. "No doubt I have died myself ten thousand times before," Whitman says in "Song of Myself" and of course he cannot mean die in the way you and I do since, literally speaking, you only die once.[37] But for Whitman death is not death. It is transformation.

This principle proved immensely comforting to Whitman. Later in "Song of Myself," Whitman addresses all the souls sickened by death:

> Down-hearted doubters, dull and excluded,
> Frivolous sullen moping angry affected disheartened
>   atheistical,
> I know every one of you, and know the unspoken
>   interrogatories,
> By experience I know them.[38]

Whitman goes on to compare these interrogatories to flukes, a kind of fish, and sympathizes with those who are subject to them: "How the flukes splash! / How they contort rapid as lightning, with spasms and spouts of blood!"[39] In the lines that follow,

Whitman orders the "bloody flukes of doubters and sullen mopers"—he means us—to "be at peace." Speaking of death, he writes, "What is untried and afterward is for you and me and all." He confesses, "I do not know what is untried and afterward, / But I know it is sure and alive, and sufficient."[40] Later, he says, "Our rendezvous is fitly appointed, / God will be there and wait till we come."[41] And in a poem he would later call simply "Faith," Whitman writes, "I do not doubt that the passionately-wept deaths of young men are provided for—and that the deaths of young women, and the deaths of little children, are provided for," and by "provided for" Whitman seems to mean taken care of, a contingency considered in advance.[42] He may have hoped his readers would also think of "providence," the care or benevolent guidance of God or nature. Death, in this way of thinking, is provident. It has been foreseen and accounted for. More than provident, Whitman speculates that death might be the *purpose* of life. In any event, since death is part of the universe, it serves *some* purpose. To speak the language of computer programming, death was not a bug but a feature. If so, and if we trust in the plan of the universe, then we should not mourn our deaths but celebrate them. In dying, and in taking new form, we participate in the laws of the universe. As he tells the one shortly to die in a poem of the same name, "I do not commiserate, I congratulate you."[43]

In sum, as Whitman writes in "Song of Myself," "It is not chaos or death . . . . it is form and union and plan . . . . it is eternal life . . . . it is happiness."[44] As many poems make clear, Whitman did not believe in a conventional Christian God. But he did believe that something—a spirit, a force—created the universe, and that death belonged to the purposes of that creation as much as life. You could count on death as reliably as you count on gravity.

V.

The poems sampled above clarify a number of ambiguities in "Crossing Brooklyn Ferry." Midway through that poem, as Whitman is considering what it is that connects him to us, he says, "I too had been struck from the float forever held in solution."[45] "Float" here refers to "the fluids of the air" we have seen Whitman celebrating in another poem, "A Song for Occupations." According to the science of the day—and ours, as it happens—the universe once consisted of a nebulous cloud of gases and dust that condensed to form the sun and planets. (Here too all thanks go to gravity.) The theory dates back to the rogue philosopher, scientist, and theologian Emmanuel Swedenborg, but it found new life in the work of the French mathematician and astronomer Pierre-Simon Laplace. (Whitman likely read of Laplace's nebular hypothesis in the Scottish journalist Robert Chambers's 1844 book of popular science, *Vestiges of the Natural History of Creation*.)[46] For nebulae, Whitman often substituted "float," though he uses both terms interchangeably. Except for occasionally varying his terms, Whitman seems to have adopted the nebular hypothesis completely.

As Whitman saw it, the nebular hypothesis also explained the origins and evolution of human life, and here too he is not too far from what astronomers today believe. The same matter— the nebular gases and dust—that formed stars and planets also formed us, formed, for that matter, everything. As Carl Sagan used to intone, "The earth, and every living thing, is made of star-stuff," and he meant that the elements that compose us (carbon, hydrogen, oxygen) were themselves formed within stars and then released into the universe when a star reached the end of its life span and blew itself up. "The cosmos," Sagan used to say, sounding very Whitmanesque, "is also within us."[47] Among other things, those elements formed our planet and the chemical life of our planet, and eventually that star-stuff evolved into me, you, Walt Whitman, everything and everyone. Each of us "had been struck from the float forever held in solution," as Whitman puts it in "Crossing Brooklyn Ferry."

As you can imagine, this view of the universe invests everyday objects with an incredible if often overlooked grandeur. Hence "the glories strung like beads on my smallest sights and hearings," as Whitman describes them in "Crossing Brooklyn Ferry."[48] Thus could objects, as he also says in that poem, function as "dumb beautiful ministers." After all, they partook of star-stuff, too. They revealed God or the spirit of the universe as much as we or anything else in the universe did. "I do not doubt but the majesty and beauty of the world is latent in any iota of the world," Whitman writes in "Faith Poem."[49] "I hear and behold God in every object," he writes in "Song of Myself," and proclaims elsewhere in that poem that "I believe a leaf of grass is no less than the journeywork of the stars."[50] "Journeywork" refers to work done by a journeyman, a craftsman; the journey work of the stars is life on Earth. For Whitman, everything traces its existence, its being and makeup, back to the stars.

For Whitman, then, it all added up. The universe followed certain laws, like gravity or the conservation of matter. The existence of those laws implied a rationally ordered universe. Therefore, everything within that rationally ordered universe, including death, must have a reason for being. Nowhere does he express this sense of death and its place in an ordered universe better than in the aptly titled "Burial Poem." "Do you suspect death?" Whitman asks his reader.

If I were to suspect death I should die now.
Do you think I could walk pleasantly and well-suited
    toward annihilation?[51]

The answer, of course, is no, because, as he puts it in the final lines of the poem:

I swear I think there is nothing but immortality!
That the exquisite scheme is for it, and the nebulous float is for
    it, and the cohering is for it,
And all preparation is for it ... and identity is for it ... and life
    and death is for it.[52]

In short, everything in the universe pointed away from death and toward life. Or, rather, further life through death.

Armed with this knowledge, the opening of "Crossing Brooklyn Ferry" now makes much more sense. Whitman begins the poem by commanding the "flood tide of the river" to "flow on!" He addresses the flood tide as a "you," claiming to watch it "face to face."[53] The first time around, the line merely seems clever. Leaning over the ship's railing looking down into the water, Whitman sees his reflection in the flood tide and can thus watch it face to face. If you think about it, though, there is more to the line than mere cleverness. Inasmuch as everything—leaves of grass, flood tides, poets—are the offspring of the stars, the same spirit of creation infuses all. Just as the stars are us, and we are the stars, so too is the flood tide us, and we the flood tide. Everything tells the same wonderful story about the universe. Everything is a dumb, beautiful minister preaching the providence and purposefulness of existence. (It does not hurt, either, that flood tides occur because of gravity.) It is possible, then, to see yourself, your face, in the flood tide, in everything. Everything is a mirror, whether it reflects or not.

As "Crossing Brooklyn Ferry" makes plain, too, these shared origins of existence obtain regardless of time, place, or distance. Brooklyn and Manhattan of 1856 may look rather different from present-day Brooklyn and Manhattan, but the same tide ebbs and flows, the same celestial laws rule the earth, and the same star-stuff infuses all of existence. That people dress differently or take different modes of transportation is negligible. We all, regardless of era, are the journey-work of the stars. We all follow the same laws of chemistry and physics, including the law that we must die. But the celestial law also confirms that we die merely to live again.

IV.

Riding the East River Ferry, sharing it with tourists looking at the skyline of Manhattan and commuters looking at the screens of their smartphones, the world, with Whitman in mind, suddenly seems like a far more magical place. Before your eyes, everything—river, skyline, tourist, and banker—glows with its inner star-stuff and beats to the pulse of universal laws.

Before climbing aboard the East River Ferry or reading Whitman so intensely, I did not give much thought to gravity, star-stuff, or our exquisitely fine-tuned universe. But when you pause to think about it, as Whitman forces you to, existence is a miracle, or whatever secular term one wants to adopt in place of miracle. And that *I* exist out of all the possible forms existence could take is more miraculous still.

Unfortunately, I truly hate to report, this vision does not necessarily make me feel all that better about death. In persuading us of the miracle of existence, Whitman may only worsen the sense of loss we feel when that miraculous existence is taken away from us, as it is at death. This is particularly the case if you remain skeptical of his intimations of immortality. In a crude way, Whitman is right about the conservation of matter. Our corpse will make good manure, and like a couple after a breakup, the atoms that compose us will move on to other things. But we are not the atoms that compose us. The atoms that compose us may survive our bodily death, but no one cares about her atoms. We care about our consciousness, what Whitman calls the "really Me," and the really Me occurs because of a particular arrangement of atoms, which, so far as I can tell, do not survive our bodily death.[54]

Here, then, is what will prevent most of us from crediting Whitman and his gospel of death. Whitman believes in a soul distinct from a body. Or, at least, a soul that is ultimately unfettered to any single body. Our bodies die, Whitman allows, but our souls survive. Today, however, this distinction is untenable. We know that our soul—our consciousness—derives almost exclusively from our bodies. If dynamite explodes before it is supposed to, driving a long iron rod through the left frontal lobe of your brain, you will be a different "really You" after the accident than you were before. And if an iron rod can change your soul, imagine what death can do to it. All of which is to say that what you and I think of as the soul—the really Me—is very much a material phenomenon. Basically, we are our brains, and our brains depend upon our living, perceiving bodies. The really Me, strictly speaking, cannot survive that loss.

So when Whitman congratulates us on our death, or insists that there is nothing but immortality, I really want to believe him. I doubt that more than a handful of us can believe him, however. We know too much. These days, when I lie in bed at night, I still think of the total emptiness forever that awaits me.

Curiously, it is not Whitman's views on mortality and immortality that console us about death, but rather his take on property, about which he also had decided opinions. Whitman believed we suffered from a "mania for owning things," and this same mania may also lead us astray when it comes to thinking about life and death.

As I discuss in the next chapter, the universe may have properties for Whitman, but property is not one of them. In his view, no one owns anything, and no one *can* own anything. His belief rests on the fact that atoms, the fundamental constituents of the universe (or what were thought so at the time), do not respect or even require the notion of property. For example, you do not even own the atoms that constitute you. When you die, "your" atoms will disperse into the chemical life of the planet, where they might become the soil out of which plants grow, then the air that someone else breathes, then part of that person, then into the atmosphere or soil, then elsewhere, on and on. But at no point does anyone own them. They came together awhile to form you. Soon enough, they will disperse and form something else. Viewed from this perspective, life on earth—and the earth itself—is just atoms in motion. None of them stops long enough to be owned. If so, Whitman believes, then we ought to be skeptical about a concept like property.

Strangely enough, this insight may help us think about death, too. Our mistake may lie in thinking of life as something we own or possess. If we think of life this way, then when we die and life is taken away from us, we feel like the victim of some injustice. We feel as if we have been robbed.

But life is not something one can or even should hope to possess eternally. Although we keep pushing the numbers beyond what anyone thought possible, and currently house about seven billion people, the earth can nevertheless only support a finite number of people at any one time. We might disagree about whether we have reached those limits, or what they are, but few would disagree that there are limits. If no one died, the earth would soon be packed cheek by jowl. If so, then for others to enjoy their share of life I must eventually relinquish mine. I cannot hope to own it indefinitely.

I find it helps to think of life as a book you borrow from the library. By this model, life, like the atoms of which it is composed, is not something we own but something we are trusted with for a brief period of time. When we have used it, when we have made of it what we will, we return it and it goes back into general circulation, at which point someone else gets to use it and make of it what she will.

I admit that this analogy only comforts so much. I do not want to return my book when it comes due or, worse yet, when it is recalled early. I very much want to keep it. I have grown to love it. But this may be where we err. We like to think that instead of a library, we find ourselves in a Barnes & Noble, and that the life we select is ours to keep. But the universe is not a Barnes & Noble. We live in a socialist universe, not a capitalist one. Our universe wants everyone to have a chance. It looks askance on those who would try to monopolize resources, especially the most fundamental resource of all, life.

When the day comes when I must die, then, and it hurtles toward me more quickly each moment, I do not want to die feeling like someone who has been mugged on the street and looks around in vain for aid and sympathy, angry that no police officer is there to restore justice or prevent the injustice in the first place. Rather, thinking of Whitman, I would like to die like an eccentric philanthropist, like someone who gives away everything he owns so that others may live. In other words, I do not want to die feeling like something has been taken from me. I want to die feeling like I am giving something back. Whitman helps us feel that. He helps us have the courage to die—and live—like someone who understands that for life to go on, life must end.

CHAPTER 2

Walt Whitman's Credit Report Looks Even Worse than Yours

> What is it that you made money? what is it that
> you got what you wanted?
> —WALT WHITMAN, "A Song for Occupations" (1855)

Today Zuccotti Park is an open, inviting patch of ground buried beneath the cavernous skyscrapers of lower Manhattan. On a recent May morning, crowds of freshly showered office workers, bubbling up from the Cortlandt Street subway station across Church Street, spilled through the park, turned down Broadway, and then streamed toward the glass and granite wonders of Wall Street proper, a few blocks away.

In the fall of 2011, Zuccotti Park looked far different. Back then it served as staging area and campground for the Occupy Wall Street protests that, thanks in part to cops with quick pepper-spray fingers, briefly captured national attention.

As I sat in the now-placid Zuccotti Park, fearful that I would be asked to move along—the park swarmed with police and security guards—I thought of Walt Whitman, and not just because I thought of him often these days, or because that morning, to make myself feel better about dying, I had traced his footsteps through Brooklyn and lower Manhattan. (Like me, Whitman would have boarded the Fulton Ferry in Brooklyn Heights, crossed the East River, exited at Pier 11, and walked west on Wall Street to Broadway. There, Whitman liked to climb aboard the omnibuses and chat with the drivers as they made their way uptown.) Today I thought of Whitman because many of those who occupied Zuccotti Park gathered there, in addition to the advertised reason of inequality, because of debt, their own or others, and Whitman, too, had struggled to pay his debts.

In late 1856 or early 1857, Whitman borrowed $200—about $5,000 today—from James Parton, an English-born biographer and husband of the then-popular American writer Sara Willis. Whitman hoped to pay Parton back from sales of the second edition of *Leaves of Grass*, which he brought out in late 1856. However, considering that the first edition of the book sold, as Whitman himself later put it, exaggerating only slightly, not a single copy, Whitman perhaps should not have let his books write checks his royalties could not cash.

In the event, the second edition of *Leaves of Grass* sold little better than the first. When the loan came due and Whitman could not pay it, Parton dispatched a family friend, the journalist and lawyer Oliver Dyer, to collect his debt. Dyer sued Whitman, and on the morning of June 17 appeared at the front door of the poet's Brooklyn home to collect the debt. Whitman, short of cash, offered to pay the debt in kind, with books and a landscape painting by the American artist Jesse Talbot. Dyer agreed, wrote out a receipt, and Whitman considered the matter settled.

Parton, however, did not. In all likelihood, Dyer never told Parton of the agreement he and Whitman reached but instead kept the books and painting for himself. In any case, Parton apparently felt that he had not been paid; in the years that followed, he eagerly spread the story of Whitman the deadbeat. Indeed, the debt would haunt Whitman for the rest of his life.[1]

After the Civil War, Whitman was appointed as a clerk in the Department of the Interior. Six months after taking the job, he was fired by the secretary of the interior, James Harlan, who did not want the author of an obscene book like *Leaves of Grass* employed in his office. Whitman's defenders rushed to his aid, but so did his detractors. Much to his annoyance, the story of his supposedly unpaid debt resurfaced in the Washington papers.[2] The debt was still on Whitman's mind as late as 1888, when he sought to explain his side of the story to his biographer Horace Traubel. "The devilish insistent thing," Whitman told Traubel, "has gone about so far: it means so little yet it is made so much."[3]

Like Whitman, many of the protesters in Zuccotti Park had debt on their minds. Many were angry with the federal government for bailing out enterprises like American International Group (AIG), which owed hundreds of billions of dollars to banks and investment houses like Goldman Sachs and therefore was thought too big to fail. (The Art Deco AIG skyscraper is a few blocks east of Zuccotti Park, the Goldman Sachs tower a few blocks west.) Some protesters were equally angry that though the federal government bailed out the likes of AIG and, indirectly, Goldman Sachs, it did relatively little for people who could not make their mortgage payments and thus faced foreclosure on their homes. Many protesters, however, especially among the young, struggled under the burden of student loans, which, as has been widely reported, in the United States now exceeds even credit card debt.[4] Like Whitman's debt, unpaid student loans would follow borrowers to their graves. Nothing, not even declaring bankruptcy, could absolve them of their student loans. Nor would death necessarily make their debts go away. You might leave the mortal plain, but if your parents co-signed your student loan, it will live on to haunt them.[5]

Of course, debt alone did not drive protesters to Zuccotti Park. After all, few complained about student loans—publicly, anyway—when the economy hummed along and a college degree all but guaranteed a good job. But when, as the Associated Press recently reported, over half of all college graduates under the age of twenty-five are unemployed or hold jobs that do not require their college degrees, then student loans can feel less like an investment in your human capital and more like an albatross around your neck.[6] Only then did private grumbling turn into public protest. That is, debts matter when you do not have the money to pay them back. And, to state the obvious, they—debts—are born when you do not have the money to buy what you need (or want) in the first place.

Inside and outside of Zuccotti Park, Americans know these two facts—lack of money and rising debt—better than they would like. Indeed, this describes almost perfectly what has happened to most people over the last few decades. Beginning in the 1980s, as more and more income went to the top percentile of earners, the income of working- and middle-class families leveled off. In order to maintain the rising standard of living they had come to expect, or merely to tread water, these families went into unprecedented debt. In 1983, for example, the bottom 95 percent of households had 60 cents of debt for every dollar of income. By 2007, they had $1.40 in debt for every dollar of income. They were living as well—or better—than ever, but they were living on borrowed money. And who lent them the money? To engage in a bit of class warfare, the rich did. That is, as the top percentile of earners grew wealthier and wealthier, they spent some of their newfound income on things for themselves (like luxury cars and second homes); they invested some of it in businesses that make and sell things (like Apple and Walmart); and, finally, they invested it in the financial sector, which, by and large, was in the very profitable business of loaning money to the rest of us.[7]

To many, this situation will seem unfair. In the past, working- and middle-class families earned their rising share of national prosperity honestly. Now, instead of receiving that income in wages, they borrowed it from the wealthy and paid—in interest— for the privilege of borrowing it. Regardless of whether it was fair or not, this shift in income and wealth from the bottom to the top was dangerous. With increased debt, the economy becomes more vulnerable to financial crisis. And when the crisis comes, as it did in 2007–2008, the economy contracts, jobs disappear, and many families default on their debts, which only exacerbates the economic crisis. Demand falls further, still more jobs disappear, and still more debts go into default.

Today, the lucky ones are in debt and fortunate to have a job, even though they may not have seen a raise in quite a while. The unlucky ones, meanwhile, are in debt, out of work, and leading lives of not so quiet desperation.

But as I say, you do not need to tell most Americans this story, since they live it every day. Debt and stagnant (or fall- ing) incomes together constitute one of the greatest sources of American malaise. As the historian Tony Judt wrote before his untimely death from Lou Gehrig's disease, "We have reentered an age of fear. Gone is the sense that the skills with which you enter a profession or job would be the relevant skills for your working lifetime. Gone is the certainty that you could reason- ably expect a comfortable retirement to follow from a success- ful working career. All of these demographically, economically, statistically legitimate inferences from present to future—which characterized American and European life in the postwar decades—have been swept away." We live, he concludes, in "fear of an unknown future."[8]

Crucially, Judt observes that we have "reentered" this age of fear, suggesting that we have been there before. And so we have. Whitman suffered through his own age of economic fear and insecurity. He took on debts he could not pay. He lost jobs, struggled to find new ones, and lived through at least three major financial crises (the Panics of 1837, 1857, and 1873). Moreover, Whitman is the first major modern American poet to be born into the working class and to have experienced its struggles—and its joys—firsthand. He is also one of the first American poets to have engaged in real estate speculation. In addition to other odd jobs, from 1848 to 1855, after he left editing newspapers, Whitman built and sold half a dozen houses in the Brooklyn real estate boom that finally crashed in 1854.[9] He thus knew the possibilities, and the perils, of playing the market—of, as he put it in "Song of Myself," "spending for vast returns."[10]

Despite this familiarity with work, workers, and, more generally, life under capitalism, critics have doubted what Whitman can offer to discussions of economics, whether of his day or ours. In particular, they have charged him with nostalgia, and, therefore, irrelevance. According to this account, Whitman imbibed his politics from the proud but vulnerable community of New York artisans in the first half of the nineteenth century. These carpenters, printers, shoemakers, wheelwrights, blacksmiths, and coopers took pride in their training and skill, which, they felt, endowed them with an economic independence that made them the ideal citizens of a democracy like the United States. Beholden to no one and nothing except themselves, they were the sturdy foundation on which the Republic rested and whose interests it should serve.

Almost as soon as it came into existence, though, that artisan republic faced an existential crisis in the rise of industrial capitalism, which threatened to turn independent artisans into exploited wage slaves. (Compare an early nineteenth-century shoemaker in his workshop to the gaggle of young women tending machines in the shoe factories that proliferated in and around Lynn, Massachusetts; or a butcher at his stall to the hordes of workers manning the disassembly lines of a Chicago packing house.) Only able to look backward, Whitman, it is charged, had no solution to the problems posed by the rise of industrial capitalism, whether poverty, alienation, the amassing of great fortunes in the hands of robber barons, or the politicians bought and paid for with those great fortunes. Whitman had no solution, that is, except to insist, over and over again, on the values he had learned as a young man: independence, equality, small property, and free trade. (By free trade, Whitman meant freedom from government-imposed tariffs, which, he and others held, insured the profits of factory owners by insulating them from foreign competition, all at the expense of ordinary workers who had to pay more for their goods.)[11] This nostalgia, his critics insist, led to nothing so much as bewilderment and mystification. On the one hundredth anniversary of the publication of the first edition of *Leaves of Grass*, one critic, Leadie M. Clark, wrote: "If America had attempted to follow the economic or political theories of Whitman, she would have foundered for want of a consistent plan."[12]

Although these critics may be right that Whitman too often offered past ideals in the face of present—and unprecedented—problems, they nevertheless overlook the remarkable insights into economics Whitman offered that remain relevant today, even as we supposedly move away from the industrial world that so befuddled and offended him. In other words, capitalism may change, but its failings remain more or less the same, and Whitman saw those failings better than most. Moreover, certain virtues—fairness, equality, solidarity, care—remain relevant regardless of what stage of development an economy happens to be in. And Whitman, perhaps better than any other poet, gives voice to those virtues. To be sure, appealing to these virtues cannot solve all of the economic problems Americans face today, but they can, I believe, point us in the right direction and give us stars, besides those of endless profit and growth, to steer by.

Not long after settling into Zuccotti Park, the Occupy Wall Street protesters set up a makeshift library. One of the first books was *Leaves of Grass*.[13] In all likelihood, few protesters read Whitman for what he could tell them about the economic system they decried. In this chapter, I argue that they should have.

I.

Before they get to the poetry, readers who pick up the first edition of *Leaves of Grass* must make their way through the "Preface," which, even for someone as devoted to Whitman as I am, is admittedly tough going. Most of the "Preface" is given over to describing the qualities and capacities of "the great poet": what he must write about, how he will write about it, what he can do for his country.[14] It has its moments, but much of it is filled with needlepoint platitudes such as "Obedience does not master him, he masters it."[15] Too often, it reads like Whitman deliberately working himself up, getting his blood going for the frenzy of poetry that will follow. Wisely, he dropped the "Preface" from future editions.

Still, beneath all the platitudes and daily affirmations, the "Preface" announces one of Whitman's great themes: the misguided pursuit of wealth. As a journalist, he had also written about that theme. In an 1846 editorial for the *Brooklyn Daily Eagle* titled "The Morbid Appetite for Money," Whitman wrote of the "unholy wish for great riches that enters into every trans-action of society, and more or less taints its moral soundness."[16] Roughly ten years later, he revisited the subject of the unholy wish for great riches in the *Leaves of Grass* "Preface," and he would explore it more fully in the poems that followed.

In the "Preface," Whitman begins by discussing the abundance of American resources, how the country "need never be bankrupt while corn grows from the ground or the orchards drop apples or the bays contain fish or men beget children upon women," but he quickly asserts that abundance alone is not enough.[17] "The large-ness of nature or the nation were monstrous," he writes, "without a corresponding largeness and generosity of the spirit of the citi-zen. Nor nature nor swarming states nor streets and steamships nor prosperous business nor farms nor capital nor learning may suffice for the ideal of man."[18]

Not only do these material accomplishments not suffice for the ideal of man, the exclusive pursuit of them may do irreparable harm to his soul. For Whitman, this discussion about prosperity and the soul unfolds around the idea of prudence: "It has been thought that the prudent citizen was the citizen who applied himself to solid gains and did well for himself and his family and completed a lawful life without debt or crime. The greatest poet sees and admits these economies as he sees the economies of food and sleep, but has higher notions of prudence than to think he gives much when he gives a few slight attentions at the latch of the gate."[19] That last phrase, "at the latch of the gate," may seem odd, but it illustrates Whitman's point. Though latches and gates have their uses—they keep people out, they mark off property—they may also distract us from other more important things: what is on the other side of the gate, for instance, or where the gate leads. Today, we might say such a person cannot see the forest for the trees, cannot see the big picture.

That sense is confirmed in what follows, perhaps the longest and most contorted sentence Whitman ever wrote, but which also sets the tone for many of the poems about money that follow. Here is the whole, gargantuan sentence:

> Beyond the independence of a little sum laid aside for burial-money, and of a few clapboards around and shingles over-head on a lot of American soil owned, and the easy dollars that supply the year's plain clothing and meals, the melancholy prudence of the abandonment of such a great being as a man is to the toss and pallor of years of moneymaking with all their scorching days and icy nights and all their stifling deceits and underhanded dodgings, or infinitesimals of parlors, or shame-less stuffing while others starve . . . and all the loss of the bloom and odor of the earth and of the flowers and atmosphere and of the sea and of the true taste of the women and men you pass or have to do with in youth or middle age, and the issuing sick-ness and desperate revolt at the close of a life without elevation or naïveté, and the ghastly chatter of a death without serenity or majesty, is the great fraud upon modern civilization and forethought, blotching the surface and system which civiliza-tion undeniably drafts, and moistening with tears the immense features it spreads and spreads with such velocity before the reached kisses of the soul.[20]

Untangled, the sentence suggests that Americans should be concerned about money up to a point, about enough to guarantee their basic needs, but beyond that their concern is misspent. Man is "a great being," Whitman writes. (His gendered language dates him here. He means men and women.) He should not abandon himself to the chaos and enervation of moneymaking, which also, inevitably, involves him in lying, subterfuge, pettiness, and greed, the "shameless stuffing while others starve."[21] Moreover, such a life robs him of his connection to the earth and to the people on the earth. A prudent life devoted to making money is a wasted life, which those who live it will ultimately regret, but only after it is too late to do anything about it. Worse still, such a life betrays civilization itself, a point Whitman leaves undeveloped but will revisit in the poems.

For now, though, note how Whitman builds these sentences in the "Preface." He speaks the language of business in order to indict it. The investment in moneymaking is a "loss"; the stocks such an endeavor "issues" are sickness and desperate revolt at the "close" of the trading day, your life; the whole enterprise of moneymaking is "the great fraud" upon modern civilization; finally, moneymaking blotches and moistens with tears the "draft"—the check—that civilization writes out. In other words, Whitman does to economic language what he expects us to do to a narrowly economic life: to redirect it toward other, higher ends.

Note, too, that all these passages unfold around a debate about prudence, what a prudent citizen does or does not believe or do. Etymologically, *prudent* and *prudence* derive from *providence* and *provide*, words made out of the Latin verb *videre*, to see. Essentially, Whitman argues that the conventionally prudent citizen—concerned only with making money—does not see far enough, does not see past the latch at the gate. "The prudence of the mere wealth and respectability of the most esteemed life," Whitman writes later in the "Preface," "appears too faint for the eye to observe at all when little and large alike drop quietly aside at the thought of the prudence suitable for immortality."[22] What to the prudent man looms large—money—is, from the perspective of eternity, all but imperceptible.

Critics debate what to make of—and how much Whitman truly believes in—these tirades against moneymaking. Some have charged him with merely giving readers what they want, and thus that the rhetoric is more calculated than sincere.[23] Others think that Whitman, despite his protests, admires the flux and exchange of the market and attempts to imbue his poetry with it.[24] To me, however, these passages sound like nothing so much as the thoughts of a man who had, for the past few years, abandoned his life to moneymaking and grown thoroughly sick of it. Recall that when he writes the "Preface," and all of the poems in the 1855 edition of *Leaves of Grass*, Whitman had become, essentially, a middleman. He hired others to construct houses, which he sold to others still. Like his father, Whitman knew carpentry, but he no longer built the houses he and his family occupied for a few months before he sold them and started over. He spent his days drawing up contracts, writing receipts, and examining titles to property.[25] For some, that life may satisfy, but you cannot imagine it satisfying Whitman. Little wonder, then, that after a few years of it, Whitman cashed out. He built his family a narrow three-story house in the Clinton Hill section of Brooklyn. (This is the last house that Whitman built and occupied that still stands. You can almost see it from the Brooklyn-Queens Expressway.)[26] And he used the rest of the money to self-publish the first edition of *Leaves of Grass*. In effect, he turned money he made from developing real estate into a full-throated criticism of a life devoted to things like developing real estate for money.

II.

In sum, then, Whitman arraigns moneymaking for several reasons. To start, Whitman believes that if all you care about is making money, you will, at some point, likely take advantage of others. Moneymaking invites immorality; it may even require it. If the only point is to make money, it does not much matter how you make it. If it entails "stifling deceits and underhanded dodgings," as Whitman put it in his 1855 "Preface," then so be it. In an 1867 essay that would eventually become the first part of his 1872 book, *Democratic Vistas*, Whitman makes the point even more brashly. "The depravity of the business classes of our country," he writes, "is not less than has been supposed, but infinitely greater."

> In business, (this all-devouring modern word, business,) the one sole object is, by any means, pecuniary gain. The magician's serpent in the fable ate up all the other serpents; and money-making is our magician's serpent, remaining to-day sole master of the field.[27]

At root, *depravity* simply means crooked, and when pecuniary gain becomes the one sole object, then other objects—fairness, justice—fall away, and some will not hesitate to behave like crooks, as we say, if the payoff is big enough. Many can—and do—come by their pecuniary gain honestly. But many, as readers of the Business section of the *New York Times* can attest, succumb to temptation and acquire their wealth dishonestly. In a talk on the Depression of 1873 that he planned but never delivered, Whitman wrote: "As in Europe, the wealth of to-day mainly results from, and represents, the rapine, murder, outrages, treachery, hoggishness, of hundreds of years ago, and onward, later, so in America, after the same token." It is "not yet so bad," Whitman was willing to grant, "or so palpable—we have not existed long enough—but we seem to be doing our best to make it up."[28]

For Whitman, however, even those who come by their wealth honestly may still be depraved. The problem may not be crooked dealings per se but rather the elevation of moneymaking above everything else one might do in life. To put it another way, the pursuit of wealth is depraved because it substitutes a means for an end. The problem is not just that pecuniary gain has become the one sole object, tempting people to behave badly, or crowding out all other possible objects, but that pecuniary gain is not a legitimate object in and of itself. At best, it is—or should be—a means to some other end.

As you will recall from the previous chapter, Whitman believes that our selves—our souls—survive our bodily death. Money, by contrast, does not. You cannot, as the phrase has it, take it with you. As a result, Whitman believes, we should not devote our lives to it. As he writes in the "Preface," we should "prefer real longlived things," not false, short-lived things like money.[29] "Only the soul is of itself," he says, "all else has reference to what ensues."[30] In other words, we should demote money from an end to a means because what ensues—our immortal souls—is almost certainly not about money. (Here, as at other times, Whitman echoes Christ: "For what is a man profited, if he shall gain the whole world, and lose his own soul?")[31] For Whitman, money is valuable to—and only to—the extent that it can enable you to pursue other ends. Whitman can be vague about what those other ends are or should be, but he is certain they are about the cultivation of your immortal soul, and equally certain they do not include making money.

Indeed, throughout a poem like "Song of Myself," Whitman is at pains to lay bare the unnaturalness of money and, more broadly, of property. "I think I could turn and live awhile with the animals," Whitman writes, "they are so placid and self-contained":

They do not sweat and whine about their condition,
They do not lie awake in the dark and weep for their sins,

They do not make me sick discussing their duty to God,
Not one is dissatisfied . . . . not one is demented with the mania
    of owning things,
Not one kneels to another nor to his kind that lived thousands
    of years ago,
Not one is respectable or industrious over the whole earth.
So they show their relations to me and I accept them;
They bring me tokens of myself . . . . they evince them plainly
    in their possession.[32]

As Whitman imagines it, among other reasons to prefer animals to people is that among animals "not one is demented with the mania of owning things." Both *demented* and *mania* derive from the Latin, *mens*, "mind," and Whitman suggests to be demented by the mania of owning things is, literally in the case of a word like *demented*, to be out of your mind. (*De-* means "out from.") In other words, in seeking to own things, we lose our minds, and we risk losing our souls.

By contrast, animals offer a different way to live. "They show their relations to me and I accept them," and their relations, crucially, do not involve property. That is, if the mania of owning things dements people, leads them out of their right minds, then animals restore Whitman to himself by reminding him of a life beyond the mania of owning things. And they illustrate this life without property even in the way they impart the lesson to Whitman. The animals show him their property-less way of life, and Whitman accepts it much as one would accept a gift from a friend. However, the gift here is not an object but a reminder that the person already possesses the gift that would be given. Nothing in fact changes hands or need change hands. The animals merely bring Whitman "tokens of myself." Moreover, they continue to possess these tokens even after they give them away. At the end of the section, these tokens remain theirs (they continue to "evince them plainly in their possession"), even as Whitman now has them, too.

It is a riddle. What can you give away and still possess? The answer: what someone has forgotten they already have. In this case, what you can give away and still possess is a new way of thinking about possession, a way of life not demented by the mania of owning things.

III.

What is that new way of thinking about possession, about owning things? What is the opposite or the absence of the mania of owning things? The answer may come in the opening lines of "Song of Myself." These lines have become so famous and famil-iar we can easily overlook their strangeness, and what they have to say about ownership.

> I celebrate myself,
> And what I assume you shall assume,
> For every atom belonging to me as good belongs to you.[33]

For many readers, these lines will grate. Together with the title of the poem, they can make Whitman seem like a narcissist. But Whitman imagines that he is no different from you or anyone else. He is merely representative. To celebrate himself, therefore, is to celebrate everyone. That is, we are supposed to read *assume* in the second line to mean "to take for granted" or "suppose," in which case Whitman is saying that what I take for granted, you also take for granted, and thus when I celebrate myself I celebrate you, too.

For the lines (and the poem) not to seem purely egotistical, we have to read them that way. But you can also read *assume* in the second line in the sense of "to seize, to claim." (If you default on your mortgage, as Whitman the house builder well knew, the bank will assume possession of your house.) Read that way, Whitman is from the outset offering a different way to think about property. In which case, to say "what I assume you shall assume" is another way of saying, "what I own you shall own." That sense is confirmed by the line that follows: "For every atom belonging to me as good belongs to you." You can read "as good" here to modify "atoms": *your atoms* are just *as good* as mine. Therefore we are equal. But you can also read it to modify "belonging": my atoms *as good belong* to you. In other words, my atoms are your atoms—or may as well be. Therefore we are literally the same. Whitman probably wants us to read his opening lines both ways—our atoms are equal and our atoms are interchangeable—but I am sure he wants us to read it this last way.

As a youth, one of Whitman's favorite books was *Ten Days in Athens* (1822), by the Scottish writer Frances Wright. The book, Whitman later told his friend Horace Traubel, "was daily food to me: I kept it about me for years."[34] The novel takes place in Ancient Greece and consists of conversations between the philosopher Epicurus and his acolytes. "Every thing," Epicurus tells one of his followers, "is eternal," and atoms prove it. "The elements composing all substances are,

> so far as we know and can reason, eternal, and in their nature unchangeable; and it is apparently only the different disposition of these eternal and unchangeable atoms that produces all the varieties in the substances constituting the great material whole, of which we form a part. Those particles, whose peculiar agglomeration or arrangement we call a vegetable to-day, pass

into, and form part of, an animal to-morrow; and that animal again, by the falling asunder of its constituent atoms, and the different approximation and agglomeration of the same—or, of the same with other atoms—is transformed into some other substance presenting a new assemblage of qualities.[35]

Later in life, as editor of the *Brooklyn Daily Eagle*, Whitman reviewed an 1847 translation of the German chemist Justus von Liebig's *Organic Chemistry in Its Application to Agriculture and Physiology*.[36] In the chapter "On the Causes which Effect Fermentation, Decay, and Putrefaction," Liebig writes: "It is evident that the active state of the atoms of one body has an influence on the atoms of the body in contact with it; and if these atoms are capable of the same change as the former, they likewise undergo that change; and combinations and decompositions are the consequence."[37]

Whether Whitman got it from Wright or Liebig, he believed that atoms bond, disband, and then assume new forms. As we began to explore in the last chapter, when you are born, atoms coalesce into you. When you die, they disperse and, ultimately, unite into something else. Not long after your death organisms in your gastrointestinal tract and respiratory system begin turning your body tissue into a potpourri of gases and fluids, whose accumulation forces other liquids in your body to seep into the surrounding environment. At this point, your atoms are free to become something, virtually anything else. Your corpse, Whitman liked to observe, will make fine manure.[38] "And now," he writes in "Song of Myself," the grass "seems to me like the beautiful uncut hair of graves."[39]

But you do not have to die to become something else. Even within the course of your life, your body constantly exchanges atoms with the world and, of course, with other people. Atoms from the carbon dioxide I exhale are absorbed by plants, and combined with water and energy from the sun, transformed into atoms of glucose for the plant and atoms of oxygen for you. In other words, someone else eventually breathes the oxygen atoms I have exhaled. Or, if someone eats the plants—or eats the animals that eat the plants—he or she does not breathe my atoms but consumes them. Either way, my atoms are as good as your atoms; in fact my atoms are now your atoms, and vice versa.

To be sure, something—some consciousness, some "us"— survives this exchange of atoms, and so Whitman believed. But for him the far more important fact is that the fundamental constituents of the universe, atoms, neither respect nor even require the notion of property. Every atom belonging to Whitman as good belongs to you. Indeed, perhaps an atom of yours did belong to him at one point, and now it belongs to you. It will soon belong to someone else. If so, then "belong" is not quite the right word to describe its relationship to you or anyone. Your atoms do not belong to you. You do not own them. No one does, nothing does. They circulate more or less freely, according to the laws of chemistry, not the law of who owns what. Whitman's point is that in our universe, no one really owns anything. "The wisest soul," he wrote in his notebook from this period, "knows that no object can really be owned by one man or woman any more than another."[40] In short, as I put it in the previous chapter, the universe has properties. But property is not one of them.

All this matters because for Whitman we need to act in accordance with these eternal, universal laws. And since the universe does not give a hoot about money or property, we err so long as we make money or property the sole object of our life, or any object at all, really. We err too if we identify with our property; if we think that anything resembling ourselves makes its way into what we own. Conversely, we succeed so long as we devote ourselves to something other than ownership or the means to ownership, money. "The greatest poet," Whitman concludes in the 1855 "Preface," "knows that the young man who composedly periled his life and lost it has done exceedingly well for himself, while the man who has not periled his life and retains it to old age in riches and ease has perhaps achieved nothing worth mentioning."[41] By contrast, "Little or big, learned or unlearned, white or black, legal or illegal, sick or well, from the first inspiration down the windpipe to the last expiration out of it, all that a male or female does that is vigorous and benevolent and clean is so much sure profit to him or her in the unshakable order of the universe and through the whole scope of it forever."[42] In other words, our best investment, the surest profit, is to forget about investments and profit in money and, instead, behave vigorously, benevolently, and cleanly. If so, Whitman writes, deliberately reworking his financial metaphor, "The interest will come round . . . all will come round."[43] If not, we have misspent our life.

IV.

In philosophical terms, Whitman is attempting to derive an *ought* from an *is* or, in the case of property, an *ought not* from an *is not*. If the universe is not about property, we ought not to make property the purpose of our lives. Although this may make a certain, immediate sense, such a strategy also has its dangers. Philosophers call it the naturalistic fallacy, or the belief that what is found in nature is inherently good and therefore worth emulating. In some cases, acting in accordance with nature may seem unimpeachably right. For example, as Whitman says in the "Preface," we should devote ourselves to "all furtherance of fugitives and of the escape of slaves."[44] For Whitman, this is one of the acts for which "the interest will come round." It is "sure profit" because it corresponds with the eternal laws of the universe. If the universe does not entail property in things, it almost certainly does not entail property in people, slaves. Therefore, we ought to help slaves free themselves.

Yet just because we follow the supposed dictates of nature or the universe does not mean we behave ethically. The problem is not so much that we may never agree on the true nature of nature, so to speak, but that even if we could, nothing says that we should behave in accordance with it. Even if we could definitively prove that nature is X, for example, it does not necessarily mean that we ought to do X. As Stephen Pinker whimsically puts it, those who fall for the naturalistic fallacy are left believing that "if birds and beasts engage in adultery, infanticide, cannibalism, it must be OK."[45] But just because birds and beasts sleep around, kill their babies, and eat one another does not mean we should follow suit. Suppose the universe is meaningless. That does not mean I should live my life accordingly. Or suppose Whitman is right, and the universe does not sanctify property. That fact alone does not mean we should all turn into communists.

Still, the fact that nature or the universe behaves in a certain way is not irrelevant to fundamental decisions about how to live our lives. It may not clinch the deal by itself, but it can coax us in some ways rather than others. If we conclude that the monomaniacal pursuit of property leads to some people behaving badly, and if we also observe that the universe has no truck with property, then we have even further cause to rethink the place of property in our lives.

Christians emphasize the short life of riches and property in this life in order to redirect attention to what matters, the long life of the hereafter. So too Whitman, who, though not a Christian, nevertheless believed that our life, like our atoms, does not come to a stop when we die. If so, then we need to keep our eyes on what ultimately matters, the development of our soul, and forget what does not matter, what we own in this life. Yet even if, unlike Christians and Whitman, you do not believe in the hereafter, this skepticism about the possibility—not to mention the sanity—of ownership may still clarify this life.

V.

If you believe, as Whitman does, that the pursuit of wealth is "the great fraud upon modern civilization and forethought," that it violates nature and the ineluctable laws of the universe, then what ought to be done? More specifically, what should you do? In the "Preface," Whitman writes, more explicitly than usual, that you should "despise riches," and it makes sense. If riches lead you astray, from your own soul and from the "real longlived things" of the universe, then look upon wealth as an enemy, as a curse. Despise it.

As much as I respect the rhetorical audacity, the injunction to "despise riches" will not do. Christianity has preached it for millennia, but lots of Christians still have exceedingly large bank accounts. Even if people could follow the advice, the sentiment potentially casts poverty in an all too flattering light. At the least, Whitman implies that resources do not matter when they clearly do. More seriously, when he says to "despise riches," he may credit people with a sentiment—the love of riches—that they do not in fact have. Although most Americans would no doubt love to be rich, and perhaps inordinately admire the rich, few of them devote their lives to becoming rich themselves. Instead, most of them seek what they—when pollsters ask them about the American dream—refer to as "financial security."[46] To be sure, their idea of "financial security" may include a lot of baubles and needless luxuries, but it hardly feels right to blame people for wanting to be financially secure.

Elsewhere, Whitman recognizes the urgency of economic security and acknowledges that simply despising riches will not suffice. In a footnote to a passage in *Democratic Vistas*, Whitman writes that his theory of democracy includes "a practical, stirring, worldly, money-making, even materialistic character," adding, "It is undeniable that our farms, stores, offices, dry-goods, coal and groceries, enginery, cash-accounts, trades, earnings, markets, & c., should be attended to in earnest, and actively pursued, just as if they had a real and permanent existence." They do not, of course, but we can pretend they do because they will help us construct the kind of democracy Whitman envisions: "Upon them, as upon substrata, I raise the edifice [of democracy]."[47] Unlike the injunction to "despise riches," then, here Whitman does not dismiss wealth or, indirectly, flatter poverty. He merely puts wealth in its place. Later in the same work, he will call for the abolition of poverty. Democracy, he writes, requires prosperity, and therefore cannot tolerate poverty. Still, as he insists, the purpose of democracy is not prosperity. Prosperity is more properly a means to an end. In order to build a functioning democracy, prosperity is necessary but not sufficient.

Although Whitman only implies this connection, the cultivation of your soul requires prosperity in the same way democracy does. Your soul, like democracy, is built on substrata of prosperity, but it is not the substrata. Even so, it cannot rise without the substrata. Only those who have money have the luxury of not worrying about money. Everyone else must scramble for it. And in scrambling for it, you neglect what matters, your soul. Just like the cultivation of a democracy, the cultivation of a soul requires an individual whose net worth is not too much, not too little, but just right.

In other words, the cruel thing about poverty is that it can make poor people care about money as much as rich people do. It can take over your life. That is why what Whitman says about money matters so much, to rich, poor, and middle class alike. Money is important, but not all-important. It matters, but other things matter infinitely more. You can chase every dollar, and account for every dollar down to the cent, so long as you recognize that dollars and cents do not make a life. They must be chased and counted for some other, better reason, some other, better life.

V.

If it is not to money or property, then to what should we devote our lives? What is that other, better reason that prosperity must serve? Another poem from the 1855 *Leaves of Grass*, eventually given the title "A Song for Occupations" in 1881, may answer that question. (As with other poems in the 1855 edition, it originally had no title.) In answering what a life should be for, the poem also reminds us what an economy, and economic life, should be for. In later versions, Whitman trimmed the poem into a more straightforward celebration of work. But in its original wildness, the first version offers something far more profound. After "Song of Myself," which is not a poem but all poems, "A Song for Occupations" may be the most remarkable poem Whitman ever wrote. "You must change your life," another poet, Rilke, writes, and Whitman's poem shows us how.[48]

The whole poem rewards close study, but, for our purposes, the opening and closing lines make the relevant point about the role of economics in our lives. The poem begins with Whitman's by now familiar remaking of the language of economics and property. Whitman writes:

> Come closer to me,
> Push close my lovers and take the best I possess,
> Yield closer and closer and give me the best you possess.
>
> This is unfinished business with me . . . . how is it with you?
> I was chilled with the cold types and cylinder and wet
>   paper between us.
>
> I pass so poorly with paper and types . . . . I must pass with the
>   contact of bodies and souls.
>
> I do not thank you for liking me as I am, and liking the touch
>   of me . . . . I know that it is good for you to do so.
>
> Were all educations practical and ornamental well displayed
>   out of me, what would it amount to?
> Were I as the head teacher or charitable proprietor or wise
>   statesman, what would it amount to?
> Were I to you as the boss employing and paying you, would
>   that satisfy you?
>
> The learned and virtuous and benevolent, and the usual terms;
> A man like me, and never the usual terms.
> Neither a servant nor a master am I,
> I take no sooner a large price than a small price . . . . I will have
>   my own whoever enjoys me.
> I will be even with you and you shall be even with me.[49]

The first thing to notice is the voice. Whitman does not ask us to come closer, or suggest that we might, but he compels us, almost commands us, to come closer. The invitation is for our own good. We will take the best he possesses, and even though we have to give him the best that we possess, we sense we have more to gain from the exchange than Whitman does. Quite simply, he possesses more of the best than we do.

But the poem also discourages us from thinking in this way, of what we can gain or lose from others. All of Whitman's puns on the language of finance—"yield," "unfinished business," "amount"—point in the same direction. Whitman is offering a different way to think about relationships with people than the usual buying and selling or who comes out ahead. Using the language of contracts, he says, "A man like me, and never the usual terms." He is not, that is, a head teacher, charitable proprietor, or wise statesman. Even less is he a boss employing a worker. All these relationships, especially boss to employee, flow in one direction only. In them, those with more—whether learning, charity, wisdom, money—confer what they possess on those with less. But if Whitman has something to offer us, he also sees much in us to take. "If you see a good deal remarkable in me," he writes later in the poem, "I see just as remarkable in you."[50] Whitman can, therefore, imagine total equality between us.

However, as the poem develops, the meaning of this opening section is not fundamental equality between you and Whitman so much as it is the "unfinished business" between you and him. Whitman, who as a young man trained and worked as a printer, here disparages print. "I was chilled with the cold types and cylinder and wet paper between us," he says, and in the next line, "I pass so poorly with paper and types." Print, Whitman implies, including his book that you hold in your hand, or my book that you now hold in your hand (or on your reading device), is a poor substitute for the man himself. The lines allow Whitman to reiterate his love for the contact of bodies and souls, but for the purposes of the poem they perform a different, even more vital role. Print is a medium. It is what comes between, in this case between poet and reader. And though what comes between can, like a bridge, connect two things, a medium is also not the thing itself, not the things that it would represent or connect. A bridge is not the land it connects. A book of poems is not the poet or the reader. In both cases, the business of genuine connection is furthered by the medium but ultimately left "unfinished."

Throughout the remainder of the poem, Whitman returns to this theme: I "send no agent or medium, and offer no representative of value—but offer the value itself."[51] Indeed, throughout the poem he is above all concerned with us not mistaking the thing—anything, really—for what it can be used or exchanged for, or how it can be represented. "The light and the shade—the curious sense of body and identity," he writes. "Have you reckoned them as mainly for a trade or farmwork? or for the profits of a store? to achieve yourself a position?"[52] They are not, Whitman implies. Things, including our bodies, are not valuable because they can be turned into something else. They are valuable in and of themselves. Nor were they made merely to be represented.

> Have you reckoned that the landscape took substance and
>   form that it might be painted in a picture?
> Or men and women that they might be written of,
>   and songs sung?
> . . . .
> Or the brown land and the blue sea for maps and charts?
> Or the stars to be put in constellations and named
>   fancy names?[53]

The answer, of course, is no. The landscape, men and women, the brown land and the blue sea, and the stars took substance and form for their own sake, and not for what they could be made into.

To put it another way, we must not mistake the thing for its representation or use because doing so puts us at risk of making what, for Whitman, is an even graver mistake: confusing things for people. Or, better said, losing sight of the fact that what matters, finally and above all else, are not things but people. Admittedly, this emphasis on the precedence of people makes the catalogue of things that occupies the middle section of the poem rather strange. The catalogue goes on and on, and includes all manner of things: occupations (farming, carpentry, sailing), yes, and the tools associated with those occupations (the shovel and pick and rake and hoe, the square and mitre and jointer and smoothing plane, the stays and lanyards, etc.), but also what Whitman calls "the closest simplest things" (the pulses of your brain, the ankle chain of the slave, what is learned in the public school) and "everyday objects" (the carpet, the snowstorm, the message of the governor, the paper I write on, the ring on your finger, the column of wants in the one-cent paper, the pay on Saturday night). In these things, Whitman writes, lies "the heft of the heaviest" and "far more than you estimated." He insists, however, that they also contain "far less" than we estimated since they do not, finally, contain you or your soul. At best, they reveal the soul. "In them," he writes, "your themes and hints and provokers."[54]

In the Gettysburg Address, Abraham Lincoln spoke of a government of the people, by the people, and for the people. Whitman would agree. In "Song for Occupations," he writes: "The President is up there in the White House for you . . . . it is not you who are here for him." And just after, "The Congress convenes every December for you," and "Laws, courts, the forming of states, the charters of cities, the going and coming of commerce and mails are all for you."[55] But whereas Lincoln spoke only of government of, by, and for the people, Whitman thinks everything is of, by, and for the people. "All doctrines, all politics and civilization exurge from you," he writes. "All sculpture and monuments and anything inscribed anywhere are tallied in you." "If you were not breathing and walking here," he asks, "where would they all be?" "All architecture," he adds, in a lovely line, "is what you do to it when you look upon it." And music, Whitman asserts, "is not the violins and cornets," it is not the instruments. Instead, "All music is what awakens from you when you are reminded by the instruments."[56]

Whitman's point is that men and women make things: governments, contracts, bibles, music, small arms and rifles, druggists' vials and jars, games of billiards and tenpins, on and on. And though, just as in "Crossing Brooklyn Ferry," those things can reveal the soul—they are dumb, beautiful ministers of the cosmos in that poem—they are not the soul. They are mediums. Or they are instruments. We err, then, when we take them to matter more than they do—or more than we do. Just as we err if we value the bridge more than the land. Without the land, the bridge would be meaningless, unnecessary, unfathomable even.

At one point in the poem, Whitman asks: "Will we rate our prudence and business so high?" "I have no objection," he answers, "I rate them as high as the highest." But even the highest thing is not higher than a person, Whitman responds. "A child born of a woman and man I rate beyond all rate," Whitman writes, again using the language of economics, "rate," to show how some things, like children, are more important than anything and, in addition, are not accounted for in the language of economics.[57] You cannot put a price on them. They are rated "beyond all rate." People matter, more than anything.

This may seem obvious, but it contains a powerful truth about economics. The final two stanzas of the poem, among the most beautiful poetry Whitman ever wrote, summarize that insight:

> Will you seek far off? You surely come back at last,
> In things best known to you finding the best or as good
>   as the best,
> In folks nearest to you finding also the sweetest and strongest
>   and lovingest,
> Happiness not in another place, but this place .. not for
>   another hour, but this hour,
> Man in the first you see or touch .... always in your friend
>   or nighest neighbor .... Woman in your mother or
>   lover or wife,
> And all else thus far known giving place to men and women.
>
> When the psalm sings instead of the singer,
> When the script preaches instead of the preacher,
> When the pulpit descends and goes instead of the carver that
>   carved the supporting desk,
> When the sacred vessels or the bits of the eucharist, or the lath
>   and plast, procreate as effectively as the young silversmiths
>   or bakers, or the masons in their overalls,
> When a university course convinces like a slumbering woman
>   and child convince,
> When the minted gold in the vault smiles like the night
>   watchman's daughter,
> When warrantee deeds loafe in chairs opposite and are my
>   friendly companions,
> I intend to reach them my hand and make as much of them as
>   I do of men and women.[58]

In the penultimate stanza, Whitman's point seems to be that if all things are the "themes and hints and provokers" of our souls, then how far away those things are does not matter. Since the universe seems to prefer common, interchangeable things like atoms, then perhaps ordinary, familiar things are best. They reveal how the universe—and, by extension, your soul—works better than unique or far-off things. And the same goes for people. Your neighbor or your mother shows you as much about humanity as anyone else. Again, perhaps far more. In any case, as Whitman says in the final line of that stanza, all else must give place to men and women. Only they matter.

The final stanza movingly illustrates that insight. Things (psalms, scripts, pulpits, and so on) do not live, people (singers, preachers, and carvers) do. And because they live, they, not the things associated with them, demand our attention. My favorite line from this catalogue of things—it must be Whitman's, too—is the last: "When warrantee deeds loafe in chairs opposite and are my friendly companions." A warrantee deed may seem too ordinary and officious to make poetry from, but it is the perfect thing to end the poem on. A warrantee deed states that the seller of a piece of real estate, and no one else, owns that property and thus has the right to transfer ownership to the buyer. It also states that the seller must defend the security of the title. For example, say that you buy a house. After the transaction, an earlier owner of the house surfaces and claims to own it. (Perhaps the person who sold it to you never paid off the original owner.) If so, its title is in dispute. The seller never had the right to sell it. In that case, a warrantee deed says that the seller—not you, the buyer—is held accountable and must pay.[59]

If you believe what Whitman has to say about property and ownership, though, there can be no such thing as a warrantee deed. No one can guarantee that he or she—and only he or she—owns anything. You do not even own your own atoms. Your chances of owning a piece of real estate are even less certain. Another owner—God, the universe, the atoms that compose the piece of real estate—will surely emerge.

But "warrantee deed" is also perfect because it hints at Whitman's recent occupation, building and selling houses, and his dissatisfaction with that way of life. Indeed, the word that follows warrantee deeds, "loafe," is a favorite of Whitman's. In "Song of Myself," in the lines immediately following those about the atoms, Whitman writes "I loafe and invite my soul, / I lean and loafe at my ease. . . . observing a spear of summer grass."[60] His point, it seems, is that warrantee deeds do not loafe; they do not have souls that can be invited or indulged. Like his other examples, warrantee deeds are not people. If they were, Whitman writes, he would grasp them by the hand and make as much of them as he does of other men and women. But since they are not, he implies, he will continue to make much—everything, in fact—of men and women. All else must give place to men and women. He rates them beyond all rate. In short, Whitman puts people first.

VI.

"Putting People First" is a cliché. It has been, I think, ever since then-governor Bill Clinton and Senator Al Gore used it as the title of their jointly published, agenda-setting 1992 campaign book, *Putting People First: How We Can All Change America.*[61] Whenever anyone, or especially any institution, claims to put people first, you can be pretty sure they do not. In any case, I would put my hand on my wallet just to be safe.

Still, I think Whitman summons this cliché back from the dead, and in doing so offers an important lesson. Instead of money or things, Whitman implies, we should devote our lives to other people. In order to make much of your soul, you must make much of other people. His poems make the point. In the final tally, Whitman devotes far more lines to celebrating others than he does to celebrating himself or things. His fascination with and sympathy for other people is boundless.

And even if, like me, you do not love people as much as Whitman does (no one does), his poem nevertheless shows us what it would mean, when it comes to economics, to put people first.

To start, we would need to remember what—and whom—an economy is for. Too often, we measure the health of an economy by gross domestic product or gross domestic product per capita. Both measure economic growth, and from a certain perspective, this makes sense. The purpose of an economy is to increase wealth. If a nation increases its wealth, it can then leave it to people to determine how to spend that wealth. If they want to invest it in real estate, fine. If they want to loan it out to others at interest, so be it. If they want to tax themselves to provide free education to all children, so much the better. Or if they want to self-publish a book of long, untitled, unrhymed poems about leaves of grass, more power to them.

It is not quite right then to say, as it is sometimes said, that our economic system, capitalism, elevates a means (money) to an end. Rather, capitalism invites nations to focus on what they can affect (the production of wealth) and leaves the ultimate ends up to individuals, who presumably know best what to do with that wealth. Capitalism says accumulate. You can worry about what to do with it after you have accumulated it. But you will not regret accumulating it.

But this approach to economics rests on two enormous assumptions, neither of which may be true. First, if we measure an economy strictly by how much it grows, we ignore the question of whether it can outgrow the earth. It remains an open question—though it closes more every day—whether our planet can support the constant growth associated with capitalism. Before long, we may deplete essential resources (like water) or, through the consumption of some resources (like oil and coal), irrevocably alter the ecosystem of the earth. In both cases, we may not just undermine economic growth but, more plainly, life as we know it. In aiming for constant economic growth, that is, we may kill the goose—the earth—that lays the golden eggs. Thus, for all else to give place to men and women, as Whitman demands, the earth that sustains men and women must come in a very close second in our economic reckoning to the men and women who live on it and make their living out of it. As the ongoing paralysis over what, if anything, to do about global warming demonstrates, that is easier said than done, but few would debate that, in the short or long term, it must be done. You cannot put people first if you have nowhere to put them.

Assuming that capitalism and constant economic growth can coexist with the earth, it may turn out that judging an economy solely by how much it grows or how much it grows per person may not be the best way to measure whether it puts men and women first. To take only the most obvious example, in seeking only to increase output or output per person, the existing approaches to economics may overlook how that output is distributed. In the last great period of economic expansion, from 2002 to 2007, the top 1 percent of earners captured 65 percent of all income growth. Worse, since the economy began to recover in 2009, the top 1 percent of earners captured 93 percent of total income growth.[62] In other words, for the majority of the population, the economy, despite growing, is not growing for them. To put it another way, just because an economy grows, or even grows per capita, it does not mean the growth is at all evenly distributed. In which case, it cannot be said to put men and women first so much as it puts some men and some women above others. Whitman would not approve.

My point here is not to debate the ins and outs of economic policy, or even, really, like protesters in Zuccotti Park, to decry economic inequality, but rather to show that Whitman reminds us that in any accounting we do, people must come first. Moreover, he gives us general principles by which to judge whether a nation, and its economy, is putting people first. Instead of measuring how much a nation produces, or even how well it distributes what it produces, we would more closely approximate Whitman's ideal by asking how much economic security it creates and distributes. Or, to phrase it another way, how well an economy enables people to forget about economics, to forget about money.

By that view, our economy, as it stands now, would surely be judged wanting. At present, more income goes to the top 1 percent of earners than at any point since the 1920s.[63] By itself that might not be so bad, but at the same time the Census Bureau estimates that 100 million people—one in three Americans—live in or near poverty.[64] And a 2011 report from the nonprofit group Wider Opportunities for Women estimated that 45 percent of Americans live without economic security. As the *New York Times* reported, that means "they are not earning enough income to cover basic expenses, plan for important life events like college or save for emergencies like unexpected health bills."[65] Whitman could not possibly approve.

I do not know what our economy will look like in fifty years. On some days I think that we can expect more of the same—with growth for the richest and stagnation and debt for everyone else. On other days, I am convinced that our widespread economic insecurity and our reckless exploitation of the planet have set us on a far more unpredictable but almost certainly regrettable path. But we can be sure that, as Whitman repeats again and again, whatever economy we invent for ourselves, the pursuit of wealth, whether by the rich or the poor, cannot be the sole purpose of life. Money and property are simply not real or long-lived enough to make pursuing them a worthwhile way to spend your time. They are a dead end.

Yet unlike with death, when we can relieve our malaise by adopting a different attitude toward it, the same approach will not work with the malaise of economic insecurity. You cannot dispel the horror of poverty by thinking differently about it. Rather, we need to ensure that others have their chance to pursue their own real "longlived" things, including working out what those real long-lived things might be in the first place. When people are in debt, as Whitman was, or when they fear for their economic security, as many of us do today, they cannot learn to despise riches and find something else, preferably someone else, to love. Whitman reminds us that the one, indisputable purpose of an economy is to make sure they can.

Was Walt Whitman Socialist?

Ain't we all socialists, after all?
—WALT WHITMAN, in conversation with Horace Traubel (1888)

L ate in his life, after he had retired to Camden, Walt Whitman received a copy of the socialist journal *To-Day*. Published in London, this July 1888 edition of the journal carried a long essay by the British writer Reginald A. Beckett titled "Whitman as a Socialist Poet."[1] "I read every word of it," Whitman told his friend Horace Traubel, "not, however, because of its literary quality (though that is respectable enough) but just to see how I look to one who sees all things from the standpoint of the socialist."[2]

As Whitman's comment suggests, he did not think of himself as someone who sees all things from the standpoint of the socialist. (Otherwise, he would not have needed to read Beckett's article.) Nevertheless, after reading the article, he was convinced, more or less, of Walt Whitman as a Socialist Poet. "I'm a good deal more of a socialist than I thought I was," he told Traubel. "Maybe not technically, politically so," he allowed, "but intrinsically, in my meanings."[3]

Frustratingly, Traubel, who was not shy about his own socialism, did not follow up with Whitman. How could one be intrinsically socialist? What does it mean to be socialist in meanings? And how did Whitman feel about being so?

The question of whether Whitman was socialist has attracted almost as much interest as the question I address later in the book, whether Whitman was gay. Unfortunately, neither question has an easy answer. Still, when it comes to the question of Whitman and socialism, at least we speak a common language. Because gay (or homosexual) was not something someone could be until quite late in the nineteenth century—technically, neither the term nor the identity existed—it is harder than it might seem to answer the question of whether Whitman was gay or not. In contrast, everyone in the nineteenth century knew what a socialist was. Whitman's favorite dictionary, the 1864 *Webster's*, defined socialism as "a theory or system of social reform which contemplates a complete reconstruction of society, with a more just and equitable distribution of property and labor."[4] That definition more or less matches the one in my edition of *Webster's*: "Any of various theories or systems of the ownership of the means of production and distribution by society or the community rather than by private individuals, with all members of society or the community sharing in the work and the products."[5]

In both these definitions of socialism, the common denominator is that everyone—rather than just someone—owns all the things (land, factories, trains) that produce or distribute other things, and therefore shares in the rewards. If we define socialism this way, Whitman was most certainly not a socialist. Although he occasionally inveighs against the rich, and often enough takes up for workers and the poor, he mentions nary a word about collective ownership. Nor did he ever affiliate himself with any of the socialist movements or parties that sprang up in the nineteenth century.

So why have so many, including in his own way the poet himself, considered Whitman a socialist? The easy answer is that after his death, Whitman, as Auden said of Yeats, "became his admirers," and most of his early admirers, especially Traubel, were socialists.[6] Naturally, they enlisted him in the cause. Yet others have also found something intrinsically socialist in Whitman's meanings. In this chapter, I review their arguments and suggest one of my own. I also offer a word about why it matters whether or not Whitman was a socialist. To put it briefly, Whitman, with his intrinsic socialism, may have staked out a more useful starting point from which to begin a conversation about contemporary economics and politics than technical or political socialism ever did, or, more to the point, could begin such a conversation today.

I.

In "Whitman as a Socialist Poet," Reginald A. Beckett admits that Whitman was by no means the ideal socialist poet. Rather, he held the position by default, for lack of any other viable candidate. Nevertheless, Beckett writes, Whitman had a fair claim to the title, for several reasons.

To start, Beckett admired Whitman's "unshakeable belief in Nature" and his "strong and fearless acceptance of the facts of life," including, as Beckett quotes Whitman, the facts of "sexual organs and acts."[7] Why should socialists care about Whitman's frank treatment of nature and sex? For socialists, such frankness meant Whitman believed in materialism, or the principle that matter undergirds and explains everything in the world. (Recall the atoms from the opening lines of "Song of Myself.") Socialists also believed in materialism, but more important, Whitman's belief in materialism bore a family resemblance to their own belief in historical materialism, which held that, in the final analysis, economics and economics alone determine nearly everything else. Similarly, Whitman believed in evolution, which, as Beckett notes, "is the foundation of Socialism," because socialists had to believe that economic systems, like species, could evolve into something else.[8]

Similarly, both Whitman and socialists believed in progress. Not just any sort of progress, either, but irresistible progress toward a more perfect society, which, for the socialists, was, of course, socialism. Whitman, who got his notion of historical development from Hegel rather than Marx, was considerably more vague about what a more perfect society would look like, but he did not doubt its advance toward perfection.

In short, for socialists like Beckett, Whitman counted as one of them because, theoretically speaking, he described the mechanics of the world—its forces and focal points—in largely the same terms as they did.

Less theoretically, Whitman shared with socialists, Beckett believed, an "insatiate love for the common people."[9] Whitman also had a perfect faith in liberty, or freedom from arbitrary control, especially the arbitrary control of autocratic and despotic governments. "When Liberty goes out of a place it is not the first to go, nor the second or third to go," Whitman writes in an early poem, "To a Foil'd European Revolutionaire," which Beckett quotes. "It waits for all the rest to go, it is the last."[10]

Whitman believed in more than just liberty, though. As Beckett recognized, liberty is what he called—in language similar to that of contemporary political philosophers—"a negative blessing."[11] That is, liberty frees you from the interference of others. It does not, however, prepare you to do anything. It merely prevents others from interfering with what you can already do or be. By contrast, political philosophers (most famously, Isaiah Berlin) described what they called positive liberty, or the form of freedom that *enabled* you to do something rather than just kept you from doing it.[12] For example, the First Amendment guarantees the negative liberty of freedom of speech. A class in public speaking, however, is a positive liberty. It enables you to take advantage of the right to free speech.

Whitman, Beckett observes, recognized that "something more [than liberty] is needed," some positive blessing, which, Beckett argues, he found in the notion of comradeship.[13] I shall have more to say about comradeship in later chapters—indeed, it figures in the discussion of whether Whitman was gay—but by comradeship, Whitman appears to have meant an abiding love for and unifying bond with other men. In short, you committed yourself to the well-being of another, and he committed himself to yours.

For socialists, comradeship looked like their touchstone, solidarity. As the International Workers of the World's slogan said, "An injury to one is an injury to all." Socialists would have thrilled, then, when they read Whitman's similar sentiment: "Whoever degrades another degrades me."[14] Newton Arvin, the American literary critic, socialist, and closeted homosexual who, seventy-five years after its original publication has still written one of the very best books on Whitman to date, found the poet's celebration of comradeship to be his greatest contribution to American life. "Out of our nineteenth-century past, out of our American past," Arvin wrote, "we inherit nothing potentially more fruitful than the vision Walt Whitman had of an all-embracing solidarity—a solidarity lifted above the level of rational conviction and political convenience to the level of sensibility, of social practice, of culture in its largest sense."[15] In his devotion to his fellow men and women, then, Whitman looked very socialist indeed.

In an 1898 article, "Whitman and Socialism," the physician
Michael Valentine Ball added two essential arguments to the case
of Whitman the Socialist Poet. First, he noticed Whitman's abid-
ing belief in the dignity of labor.[16] (See, for example, Whitman's
popular poem, "I Hear America Singing," with its mechanics,
carpenters, masons, boatmen, shoemakers, wood-cutters, moth-
ers, young wives, and girls each "singing what belongs to him
or her and to no one else.") Second, and equally important, Ball
singled out Whitman's devotion to equality. Each of us, Whitman
believes, whether prostitute or president, is composed of the same
divine material. (Again, recall from the opening lines of "Song of
Myself" that every atom belonging to Whitman as good belongs
to you. Those atoms, Whitman believed, came from God, or
whatever name one adopted for the creative force that brought
the universe into existence.) Because we share these fundamen-
tal constituents of being—star-stuff, as Carl Sagan called it—it
made no sense to claim that anyone was intrinsically better than
anyone else or had more or less right to anything on earth than
anyone else. "By God," Whitman writes in "Song of Myself," "I
will accept nothing which all cannot have their counterpart of
on the same terms."[17] Arvin, for his part, noticed this element of
Whitman, too. For Whitman, Arvin wrote, equality mainly signi-
fied "the equal consciousness on the part of all men of the dignity,
the distinction, the irreducible *value* of individual being, of each
man's individual being, whoever he might be."[18]

Since Beckett's article in 1888, the arguments for Whitman
as a socialist have not changed all that much. Perhaps there has
been a little less emphasis on materialism, and a little more on
comradeship, but the case has essentially remained the same.
Whitman believed in liberty and democracy, and still more
important, he believed in equality and solidarity. He preached, as
Arvin put it, "the gospel of comradeship."[19]

To these arguments, I would only add that if Whitman is a socialist, he is a socialist in much the same way that Jesus was. Like Whitman, Jesus blessed and encouraged the poor. Like Whitman, he warned that the desire for riches would lead you off the path toward God. And like Whitman, he preached universal love. Like Jesus, too, Whitman had a vision of the creation, and how what you did on earth could honor the essential virtues of that creation.

II.

So was Walt Whitman a socialist? Is the socialist part of my subtitle deserved?

As usual, you do well to trust what the poet himself said. He was not technically or politically a socialist, but intrinsically, in his meanings and from a contemporary political perspective, that may be the very best kind of socialist to be. As I describe in the previous chapter, when it comes to thinking about the economy, Whitman gives us certain ideals—fairness, equality, solidarity, care—that, he believes, a just society would bring into being. He does not tell us *how* to bring those ideals into being or what political or economic system would best bring them into being, only that a just society could not exist without them. In his day, socialists believed that collective ownership offered the best way to fulfill those ideals. Few agree with them today, and we may well have to find a new way. That does not, however, mean the ideals are any less valid.

This, anyway, is what I take Whitman to mean when he asked, "Ain't we all socialists, after all?" The context for the question, which is really more of an assertion disguised as a question, was another conversation with Horace Traubel. In March of 1888, the poet was paid a visit by the English writer and socialist Ernest Rhys. (Rhys was also the founding editor, God bless him, of the Everyman's Library, which sought to bring the classics to the masses.)[20] While visiting Whitman, Rhys apparently went on about William Morris, the English artist, writer, and prominent socialist. "Do you have any sympathy for the socialism of these men?" Traubel asked Whitman after Rhys had left. "Lots of it— lots—lots," Whitman replied. He elaborated on the thought:

> In the large sense, whatever the political process, the social end is bound to be achieved: too much is made of property, here, now, in our noisy, bragging civilization—too little of men. As I understand these men they are for putting the crown on man— taking it off things. Ain't we all socialists, after all?[21]

By political process, I take Whitman to mean the way socialists would bring about their socialist system (by, say, voting for it) as well as the system (collective ownership) itself. If so, then Whitman seems to say that the political process, the means, do not matter. What matters is the end: putting the crown on man— putting people first, as I described it in the previous chapter—and taking it off things. Perhaps collective ownership of the means of production is necessary to put the crown on man and take it off things, but perhaps it is not. Some Scandinavian countries have come close enough to the mark, I think, without bothering with collective ownership, and some of our own welfare programs (Social Security, to name but one) put people above things by guaranteeing everyone access to enough things, regardless of who owns what, to keep them decently alive. In other words, the process matters less than the result.

Traubel, however, ever the socialist, was not satisfied with Whitman's answer. "But about their political program—how about that?" he asked the poet. Whitman did not bite. "Of that I'm not so sure," Whitman responded. "I rather rebel. I am with them in the result—that's about all I can say."[22]

To Traubel, Whitman had to apologize for his reservations about the political program of socialists. Today, though, his reservation may not require an apology. In fact, it might be a redeeming feature. Many of us, including more Americans than would ever think of themselves as socialists or spend a single minute thinking about the collective ownership of the means of production, are nevertheless, like Whitman, with the socialists in the result. We too want to put the crown on man and take it off things. We may disagree about how to do so, but Whitman, intrinsically socialist, and socialist in his meanings, reminds us why we want—and should want—to do so. The lives of *all* men (and women) matter, not the things they may acquire or accumulate. To that extent, Whitman was right. We may all be (or have it in us to be) socialists, after all—including him.

CHAPTER 3

With Walt Whitman, Making It Rain

Sex, sex, sex.
—WALT WHITMAN, in conversation with Horace Traubel (1889)

In the late 1850s, Walt Whitman wrote a series of poems celebrating what he called "manly love," the love men had for other men.[1] Whitman included the poems in the 1860 edition of *Leaves of Grass* under the heading "Calamus," a plant with a suggestive, phallic-shaped flowering spike growing out of it. As I discuss in the next chapter, the exact nature of this manly love— essentially, whether it involved genitals or not—remains very much unsettled. In any case, Whitman wanted a series of poems that would counterbalance the "Calamus" ones. Whereas "Calamus" would celebrate the love of men for men, these new poems would celebrate the erotic love between men and women. The poems, Whitman imagined, would be "full of animal fire, tender, burning,—the tremulous ache, delicious, yet such torment. The swelling elate and vehement, that will not be denied."[2] To assemble the series, which he eventually called "Children of Adam," Whitman gathered three poems from the 1855 and 1856 editions of *Leaves of Grass*, including the justly famous "I Sing the Body Electric" and the perennially controversial "A Woman Waits for Me," and wrote another dozen shorter poems.

Among these shorter lyrics is the eighth poem in the series, later given the title "Native Moments." By "native," Whitman means a couple of things: inborn or innate, but also simple, natural, without affectation—possibly even uncivilized. To put it simply, he is talking about moments of overwhelming sexual desire, which, he believes, are native (instinctual) to us and native (almost crude) in and of themselves. Either way, these moments cannot and should not be denied. Whitman writes:

> Native moments! when you come upon me—Ah you
>   are here now!
> Give me now libidinous joys only!
> Give me the drench of my passions! Give me life coarse
>   and rank!
> To-day, I go consort with nature's darlings—to-night too,
> I am for those who believe in loose delights—I share the
>   midnight orgies of young men,
> I dance with the dancers, and drink with the drinkers,
> The echoes ring with our indecent calls,
> I take for my love some prostitute—I pick out some low person
>   for my dearest friend,
> He shall be lawless, rude, illiterate—he shall be one
>   condemned by others for deeds done;
> I will play a part no longer—Why should I exile myself from
>   my companions?
> O you shunned persons! I at least do not shun you,
> I come forthwith in your midst—I will be your poet,
> I will be more to you than to any of the rest.[3]

In many of his poems, Whitman defiantly takes up for slaves, prostitutes, and assorted social outcasts. In this poem, he takes up "for those who believe in loose delights," for the young men who engage in "midnight orgies." Whitman vows to become the poet of these young men because he wants to include everyone—and everything—in his poetry, especially those whom others look down upon. In addition to including them, though, he also wants to rescue these young men and their rampant lust from the reproach of others. The young men are "nature's darlings," Whitman writes. Nature loves them and their passions as much as any other person or passion. More, you might say, since nature—and the propagation of the human species—depends on these passions.

But Whitman does more than just defend these young men. He identifies with them—and writes poems devoted to "libidinous joys only"—because he too is susceptible to these overwhelming desires. These are "native moments," and as a part of nature himself, Whitman also experiences them. As he announces in the first line, they come upon him as well. To insist otherwise, Whitman suggests, is to "play a part," to pretend to be someone he is not, to pretend that he is not occasionally overcome by sexual passion. It is also to "play *apart*," to separate, "exile," himself from his natural companions, male and female. I am, Whitman insists, no better than (and as good as) these young men on their midnight orgies.

Although it may seem tame to us, in its own day the poem—and others like it—could shock. Whitman's most illustrious reader, Ralph Waldo Emerson, walked with the poet through Boston Common in 1860 and advised him against publishing poems like "Native Moments" in the third edition of *Leaves of Grass*. Emerson did not mind the poems, but he thought they would scare off readers. Whitman listened thoughtfully and then politely ignored the advice.[4] Poems like "Native Moments" would also get *Leaves of Grass* literally banned in Boston. In 1882, the Boston district attorney declared the 1881 edition of the book obscene.[5]

In choosing to write about sex, though, Whitman insisted he had no choice at all. After the Boston district attorney banned *Leaves of Grass*, Whitman published an essay defending himself and his book. "I could not," he wrote, speaking of *Leaves of Grass*, which he thought of as one long poem, "construct a poem which declaredly took, as never before, the complete human identity, physical, moral, emotional, and intellectual (giving precedence and compass in a certain sense to the first), nor fulfil that *bona fide* candor and entirety of treatment which was a part of my purpose, without comprehending this section also."[6] In other words, if Whitman wanted to write about the complete human identity, he could not ignore something as essential to our identity as sex. "Sex, sex, sex," Whitman near the end of his life told Horace Traubel, "whether you sing or make a machine, or go to the North Pole, or love your mother, or build a house, or black shoes, or anything—anything at all—it's sex, sex, sex: sex is the root of it all: sex—the coming together of men and women: sex, sex."[7]

In this chapter, I listen for what Whitman has to say about sex, the root of it all. I also listen for what he has to say about bodies, the soil of the root of it all, as it were. My hope for reading Whitman so closely, here and throughout this book, is that he can relieve us of our malaise. Unlike death and money, however, where the source of that malaise is obvious enough—we have too much of the former and not enough of the latter—our malaise about sex is less obvious. In his day, Whitman thought his contemporaries suffered from a general unwillingness to speak frankly about sex and bodies. "How people reel," he told Traubel, "when I say father-stuff and mother-stuff and onanist and bare legs and belly! O God! you might suppose I was citing some diabolical obscenity. Will the world ever get over its own indecencies and stop attributing them to God?"[8] Whitman's wish would seem to have come true. In many respects, our world *has* gotten over its own indecencies and its own unwillingness to speak frankly about sex and bodies. Wander into any bookstore and it will doubtless have at least one wall of books devoted to Human Sexuality. And at Penn State, where I teach, students can take any number of courses about the subject, and even minor in Sexuality and Gender Studies. The same is true elsewhere. Or consider popular culture, where what used to be considered indecent is now mined for our entertainment. All told, indecencies would seem to be few and far between.

But too much can be concluded from this superficial flaunting of indecencies. In the world out there, in libraries and classrooms, on television and in best-selling erotic novels, indecencies may seem like a thing of the past. But in our own heads, I believe, and about our own bodies, where it matters, indecencies—things that cannot be said or thought or done—still abound. We may no longer attribute them to God, and they may no longer quite make us reel, but they endure nonetheless. Our sense of shame, that is, is alive and well. (Mine is, anyway, as I discovered in the course of writing this chapter.) Moreover, as Whitman knew, shame keeps us from realizing the splendor of our bodies and the grandeur of our desire. More than anything else, Whitman tries to absolve us of that shame and reconnect us to the miracle of bodies and the torment yet deliciousness of sex. It is a lesson we can still stand to hear.

At the same time, Whitman and other partisans of the sexual revolution may have succeeded all too well. If shame is one source of our malaise, the absence of any shame about our sexuality, what we might call our shamelessness, is doubtless another. By shamelessness, I mean our tendency to treat our bodies—and others'—as machines for the fulfillment of our pleasure. Alas, Whitman occasionally encourages this shamelessness. At his best, though, he reminds us how we might navigate between these two perils: the sin of shame and the equally hazardous sin of shamelessness.

I.

Here is how I wound up at a strip club in the foothills of the Allegheny Mountains.

Before Whitman or anything he wrote can help us, we need to figure out what is wrong with us, and then whether what he has to say is of any use. So, when it comes to sex, what ails us, and what does Whitman propose doing about it? In each of the previous chapters, I am helped along in this search by retracing Whitman's steps and re-creating what inspired him, hoping not just to understand the poems better but also their contemporary relevance. In the first chapter, I boarded the Brooklyn Ferry, thereby reliving the scene that gave birth to some of Whitman's profoundest thoughts about death. In the second chapter, I followed Whitman from Brooklyn, where he built houses and took out an ill-advised loan, across the East River, through Wall Street, to Zuccotti Park, where our own generation made its stand against what Whitman called the toss and pallor of moneymaking. A chapter on sex, however, especially one that begins with a poem like "Native Moments," throws a wrench into this approach. Even if I did not love my wife as completely as I do, I could not, in good conscience, take for my love some prostitute, as Whitman boasts he will do. In addition to being illegal in all but one state, prostitution, to put it mildly, creates certain ethical dilemmas.

So what to do? How can one share in the midnight orgies of young men without getting arrested or breaking up a marriage? How can we not just read but in some way experience what

Whitman has to say about sex? After some thought, it hit me, as if God Himself had revealed it. A strip club! More specifically, the End Zone Show Club in beautiful Port Matilda, Pennsylvania. Its website boasts that it is "Home to Central Pennsylvania's Hottest Dancers!" Also, that it has a free shuttle from State College. Free shuttle? Sold.

Indeed, where better to dance with the dancers, to drink with the drinkers, to make indecent calls and have them echoed back to me? Where better to find the shunned persons and come forthwith in their midst? Where better to gaze at and celebrate healthy bodies, which Whitman does so often—and encourages us to do—in his poetry? Where better, that is, to understand what Whitman has to say about sex and the body and whether what he has to say is of any use to us today? Strip clubs may be old hat to you, but not me. They retain their air of the illicit and seamy. In short, they make me a little queasy. Except for a compulsory visit to one for a friend's bachelor's party about a decade ago, I have mercifully been excused from the places. Something must indeed be wrong with them, then; or, something must be wrong with me for believing that something is wrong with them. In any case, I believe they hold a key to understanding contemporary sexuality. So off I went.

For company on my excursion to the strip club, and for general moral support, I, like Whitman, picked out some low person for my dearest friend, in this case, my real friend Tom. (I have changed his name, though he claims not to care one way or the other.) Tom, it turned out, had more experience with strip clubs than I did. (He had an old girlfriend who was into them.) Together, we made a shabby—though I hoped passable—pack of nature's darlings.

Tom and I have jobs and families, which makes it difficult to get away to a strip club when the impulse strikes, especially if we also want to get any sleep that night. (I confess that I kept putting it off, too.) As a result, we did not make it to the End Zone until the off-season, so to speak. It was May, classes had ended, and most of the Penn State students and alumni who, apparently, patronize the End Zone had gone home for the summer. After we paid the cover charge, we wandered into a dimly lit though surprisingly clean room about the size of a large lecture hall. Four poles dropped from very high ceilings. Chairs lined the dance pits and walkways. Loud music played.

Unlike many strip clubs, the End Zone makes its money off the cover charge ($20 for men, $10 for women) and not by selling overpriced drinks. In fact, the beer, served on a patio, is free, but no alcohol is allowed in the club proper. On the night we came, about half a dozen men were gathered around a single dancer. As we made our way to the patio bar, the dancer was cradling a man's head between her breasts. This surprised me—I did not realize the dancers would touch you—but it turned out to be not at all unusual.

After Tom drank a beer, we returned to the club and took our seats, probably farther from the action than was polite. A dancer—perhaps Crista, possibly Felony, it was hard to keep track of their pseudonyms—was sliding around the pole, naked as the day she was born. If that had been the extent of it—naked women dancing at a respectable distance in front of you—I probably would have enjoyed myself more than I did. What straight man, in his heart of hearts, does not like to look at naked women? But it turns out that I do not really know how strip clubs work. Dancers do not stay at a respectable distance from you. Instead, the custom is to put a dollar bill on the ledge in front of you, and, sooner or later, the dancer will make her way over to where you sit and perform for you alone, up close. You are not allowed to touch her, but she is very much allowed to touch you. Or splay in front of you. Or take your dollar bill in unusual ways.

Primed by Whitman's "Native Moments," I tried to be for those—and one of those—who believe in the loose delights of the strip club. But that was all talk. In reality, I felt nervous as a zebra in a tiger pit, and I never entirely shed my unease. I had special trouble when the dancers directed their attention to me, personally. I could not look the women in the eyes, even though they look you in the eyes, nor did I feel quite right looking directly at the parts of their body offered up for my inspection. We spend our whole lives carefully covering up those parts. With good reason, we euphemistically refer to them as our privates. Because they are private. No one should have to display them in public, least of all for money, and it seemed wrong to watch the dancers disgrace themselves. The dancers themselves seemed to feel no shame or disgrace, but I could not quite get over the feeling that they should. I could never do what they do, so I thought no one should ever have to, either. Anyway, staring would only make things worse.

Tom and I stayed an hour, maybe longer, mostly out of a sense of scholarly duty. If we had stayed longer things might have gone better, as I grew not exactly more comfortable but perhaps less uncomfortable as the night wore on and I figured out how things worked. Even so, my "native moment" never came upon me, or, if it did, it came and went quickly. My "libidinous joys only" were neither particularly libidinous nor joyful, and the drench of my passions couldn't have put out a match. Here was life coarse and rank, here were loose delights, and instead of seizing them, as Whitman bid us to, I squirmed. Throughout the night, on a wall-mounted television behind the stage, the Pirates played the Brewers, and from time to time I had to remind myself to watch the dancers and not the game. That was not because I like baseball so much—though the Pirates would make the playoffs that year—but because it seemed less indecent to watch the game than it did to watch the naked woman in front of me humping the stage.

What came between me and my native moments? Why have I not been back to the strip club? I could blame feminism. No one earns an advanced degree in any humanities discipline these days without reading deeply in feminist theory. Simone de Beauvoir, Betty Friedan, Kate Millet, Laura Mulvey, Andrea Dworkin—the list goes on, and none of them would have much good to say about strip clubs, and rightly so. Dworkin, in particular, would have relished the role of killjoy. For Dworkin, pornography, which would include the degrading display of female bodies at a strip club, "creates hostility and aggression toward women, causing both bigotry and sexual abuse."[9] And you cannot very well enjoy the loose delights of a strip club if, in the back of your mind, you believe that those delights share something with the instincts of the man who beats his wife, the boss who sexually harasses his employee, or the predator who rapes an acquaintance. Feminists, and I consider myself one, will never much relish tucking dollar bills into a stripper's G-string or, as one patron did, crumbling up dollar bills and throwing them at a woman as she roiled on the checkerboard floor.

It surely did not help to loosen my delights, either, that as a Marxist, I could never quite forget the economic forces guiding the dancers in front of me. Essentially, strippers work for tips, those dollar bills we tuck into their G-strings or crumple up and throw at them. Instead of receiving a wage, many dancers in fact pay the club for the privilege of stripping. To be sure, women (and men) who cut hair oftentimes strike a similar bargain, but somehow stripping seems worse, even if the pay is better. In any case, for Marxists, every dollar tucked into every G-string provides an immediate illustration of the exploitation of labor. I did not ask the question, but I assume that few of the dancers at the End Zone worked there because they felt a calling for taking off their clothes in front of strangers or dancing suggestively in their laps. Nor, I gather, were any of them independently wealthy. Rather, they worked at the End Zone because they needed money, and few jobs, assuming they could even find a job in this economy, paid as well as taking their clothes off for strangers. The owners of the strip club, and indirectly, the patrons of the strip club, including me, all take advantage of their economic insecurity.

Still, I do not think that my feminist and Marxist sympathies can fully explain my lackluster trip to the strip club. Indeed, they probably let me off far too easily. In appealing to them, I can flatter myself into thinking that I am better than the dismal, barbaric patrons who pay for lap dances and ignore the ethical implications of what they do. I do not mean that the feminist or Marxist critiques of strip clubs do not have some truth to them. Only that, if I were being honest with myself, something else put a damper on my outing to the strip club than feminism or Marxism.

Ultimately, I think I did not have fun at the strip club because I did not want to be seen as someone who could have fun at a strip club. Because if you did have fun at a strip club, that would mean that in some sense you were in thrall to your desire, that you had surrendered your reason and your ideals to your lust. To have fun at a strip club would mean admitting that your libido trumps every other card in your hand; that you are more a desiring machine than a thoughtful human being. And among the crowd of educated, liberal, upper-middle class professionals with whom I work, gossip, and organize play dates, you can admit to almost everything else except overwhelming sexual desire. Try it. At the next dinner party, start telling the story of the funny thing that happened to you on the way to the strip club. Or the wild thing you saw on the Internet last night when you were looking at pornography. See if you are invited back.

In retrospect, part of me envies the other men at the strip club, who did not apologize for their lust. By contrast, I could do nothing but apologize for mine, so much so that I apologized it right out of existence. Some of those apologies may have been called for. The feminists and Marxists are right. Some lust does do more harm than good. But so does pretending that you do not lust, ever, or that you have complete control over it. Because if you do have complete control over it, it ceases to be lust at all. And here is where Whitman can help us. He insists, in poem after poem, that an innocent, even healthy form of lust must exist. Perhaps its finest expression is not found in strip clubs, but it must exist somewhere, and it would be surprising if it made no appearance whatsoever at a strip club. Whitman reminds us that we do not want to live in a world without lust, one without libidinous joys, and we certainly do not want to be the sort of person who cannot acknowledge these passions in himself (or, of course, herself).

In other words, those *are* some of Central Pennsylvania's Hottest Dancers, and if you cannot admit that, something is wrong.

II.

Tom and I drove to the End Zone rather than take the free shuttle. I calculated that if we needed to leave quickly, we would not want to have to wait for a shuttle. Now that I think about it, though, it seems odd that Tom and I did not take the End Zone shuttle. (After all, aren't liberals supposed to love public transportation?) But I imagine one of the reasons Tom and I drove to the strip club rather than take the shuttle is that the shuttle would have to stop in downtown State College. And even after classes let out, downtown State College still swarms with students, alumni, and God knows who else. Someone—one of our students, one of our colleagues, one of our friends—might see us blithely climbing aboard the shuttle, and we would suddenly have to worry about what they thought. Actually, we would know exactly what they thought, and what we would feel. They would feel contempt, and we would feel shame. Pure, unadulterated shame. Because, as I suggest above, we would have been caught in a moment of lust, of libidinous joys only.

Or consider this less hypothetical example. In preparing to write this chapter, I went to the campus library and tracked down an armful of textbooks about contemporary sexuality. I wanted to see what students today learn in their human sexuality classes. While waiting in line to check out the books, I ran into a colleague from the English department. Chatting about our plans for the summer, I did everything I could to keep the stack of sex books tucked discreetly behind me, covers down, out of sight. I could not bear for her to see me with them. I suppose I could have explained why I was checking the books out of the library. ("They're for research, I swear!") But that an explanation would be required is my point. In the absence of one, I would just be some pervert checking smut books out of the library. I would have, that is, been ashamed. The blood would rush to my cheeks, my palms would sweat, and I would want to get the hell out of there as quickly as possible.

Shame is a strange emotion. One of its earliest and, arguably, best theorists was Aristotle. For Aristotle, shame occurs when someone (me) does something (check dirty books out of the library) that brings him into disgrace in the eyes of someone else (my colleague). A sort of "pain and agitation," Aristotle writes, inevitably follows.[10] Aristotle offers a number of examples of acts that inspire shame: cowardice; refusing to pay back a loan;

profiteering; stinginess; flattery; softness; smallness of mind and meanness; boastfulness; ignorance; poverty; taking money for sex; and, oddly, being sexually violated, "for submission and lack of resistance comes from effeminacy or cowardice," Aristotle helpfully explains, thereby blaming the victim.[11] In his discussion of shame, as the cowardly victim of rape suggests, Aristotle returns again and again to the subject of sex, which, perhaps with the exception of what to do with our bodily waste, is what most often shames us. In particular, Aristotle singles out licentiousness as particularly likely to inspire shame, and defines it as "having sexual relations with those with whom one should not or where one should not or when one should not."[12] In other words, we are ashamed when we let our lust triumph over our good sense.

For Aristotle, shame, like board games, takes at least two: the person who does something shameful and the person who witnesses or learns of that misbehavior. Indeed, Aristotle devotes as much space to *whom* one is likely to feel shame in front of as he does to what will inspire shame in the first place. Basically, you feel shame in front of those you admire or who, until recently anyway, admired you. (You also feel shame, Aristotle notes, in front of those who like to gossip and those who make their living by making fun of other people. Today he would just say bloggers.) Conversely, Aristotle argues, you do not have to worry about feeling shame before babies and small animals, mostly because they cannot speak, but also because they do not have big enough eyes in which you could see your shameful actions reflected.[13] Aristotle's point is that shame is social. Unless someone sees me board that shuttle, or sees me tuck a dollar bill into a G-string, I am not likely to feel shame.

But here Aristotle may go wrong. Or so Sigmund Freud would say. Freud, who is more useful as a philosopher than a scientist, had a slightly more complicated take on shame than Aristotle. He held that shame, ironically, comes not from what others think of us but from what we think of ourselves, from our excessive love of ourselves, what he called our narcissism. As children, Freud argues, we innocently and unreservedly love our whole beings, including and especially our bodies. When she was two years old, for example, our daughter loved to run around the house with no clothes on, shouting, with pure joy, "I'm naked!" Part of becoming an adult, however, is learning to direct that self-love outward toward others. (Homosexuals, Freud imagined, in his half-cocked way, failed to make this transition. They loved others of the same gender because they really just loved themselves.) We may learn to love others, Freud argues, but we never give up that original and immensely gratifying love of ourselves, and as adults we seek to re-create it. To do so, we construct what Freud calls an ego ideal.

As we develop, our parents, educators, and friends tell us what is right and what is wrong. Our ego ideal is the embodiment of what is right. Our ego ideal, as Freud writes, is "possessed of every perfection that is of value."[14] It is just, honorable, merciful, and brave. We build up a perfect version of ourselves so that we might fall in love with it. And our conscience, to the best of its ability, guards the sanctity of this ego ideal, which is to say it guards our capacity to love ourselves. If we have desires that would in any way mar our opinions of our perfect selves, our conscience represses those desires and directs them toward other, more appropriate activities. To return to my daughter, she will soon learn—even if we never teach her—that running around naked is clearly wrong and that she will have to give it up. As an adult, her ego ideal, influenced by these worldly beliefs, will be much more discreet. And she will love herself for that sense of discretion. Moreover, if she ever feels the impulse to celebrate her naked self again, the impulse will be repressed or channeled in other directions. Perhaps she gets a pedicure or buys a new dress, which will briefly, but more appropriately, allow her to admire her body again.

Our conscience, however, is always fighting a losing battle against our desires. Some desires slip past its defenses, and we do things we should not. Perhaps we run around naked after all. Or perhaps we have sex with someone whom we should not or where we should not or when we should not. The result, Freud concludes, is shame. Not because, as Aristotle has it, we have disgraced ourselves in the eyes of others, but rather because we have disgraced ourselves in our own eyes. We have violated our ego ideal; it is no longer quite so ideal. As a result, we have made it impossible, for the moment anyway, to love ourselves. In short, shame is what comes between us and our narcissism, but it also comes about because of our narcissism.[15]

As batty as he can occasionally be, Freud nevertheless explains why I had such an anxious time at the strip club. If I had had a good time, I could not live with myself afterward. No one else who mattered saw me there. (Tom, in on the joke, does not count.) But I saw me there, and the ideal me does not go to strip clubs, pay to see naked women, or otherwise indulge his lust. That way lies shame, and my conscience battled those impulses like Popeye fighting off an army of goons.

III.

Shame, and whether it comes from how others view us or how we view ourselves, mattered a great deal to Whitman. More than anything else, his poems about sexuality and the body wage an intense, inspired war against shame. Perhaps the most famous example comes from "Song of Myself." Relatively early in the poem, Whitman is surveying all the people who, in the course of the poem, he will imagine himself as, or, as he puts it, with whom he will "merge." These include the little one who sleeps in its cradle, the youngster and the redfaced girl who turn aside up the bushy path, the suicide who sprawls on the bloody floor of the bedroom, on and on, offering what amounts to a guided tour through the personages and scenes of mid-nineteenth-century America. Midway through the catalogue, though, Whitman stops and, out of nowhere, declares:

> Twenty-eight young men bathe by the shore.
> Twenty-eight young men, and all so friendly.
> Twenty-eight years of womanly life, and all so lonesome.

By the way, if, in addition to malaise about sexuality, you feel malaise about writing good unrhymed poetry, Whitman can also help. Notice in this passage how he mixes repetition and variation to achieve a powerful, unexpected effect. The lines begin the same way, with the number twenty-eight, but they take divergent paths. In the first two lines, twenty-eight counts out the number of friendly young men. In the third line, however, twenty-eight counts out the years of lonely womanly life. Same number, but it refers to very different lives. Still, because the lines have a parallel construction, each beginning with twenty-eight, Whitman hints at the connection that nevertheless ties the twenty-eight young men to the twenty-eight-year-old woman. (The same thing happens with the phrases "and all so friendly" and "and all so lonesome." Each phrase has a different content, but the underlying form is the same.) Within these lines, then, Whitman establishes the vast differences between the twenty-eight young men and the twenty-eight-year-old woman, but

also, because they are described using the same sentence struc-
ture, what they share. The twenty-eight young men may seem
like they belong to a different world than the twenty-eight-year-
old woman, but, as the remainder of this section shows, they
have a fantastically intimate relationship.

In the lines that follow, one of the most remarkable passages
in all of American poetry, Whitman describes the twenty-eight-
year-old woman as she spies on the twenty-eight young men
and fantasizes, as one critic has put it, "about group sex in the
open air."[16]

> She owns the fine house by the rise of the bank,
> She hides handsome and richly drest aft the blinds of
>   the window.
>
> Which of the young men does she like the best?
> Ah the homeliest of them is beautiful to her.
>
> Where are you off to, lady? for I see you,
> You splash in the water there, yet stay stock still in your room.
>
> Dancing and laughing along the beach came the twenty-
>   ninth bather.
> The rest did not see her, but she saw them and loved them.
>
> The beards of the young men glistened with wet, it ran from
>   their long hair,
> Little streams passed all over their bodies.
>
> An unseen hand also passed over their bodies,
> It descended tremblingly from their temples and ribs.

The young men float on their backs, their white bellies swell
    to the sun . . . . they do not ask who seizes fast to them,
They do not know who puffs and declines with pendant
    and bending arch,
They do not think whom they souse with spray.

Notice how Whitman subtly but constantly switches perspective. In the first two lines, we join him as he watches the woman hiding behind the curtains of her house. Whitman then poses a question, "Which of the young men does she like the best?" His response, "Ah the homeliest of them is beautiful to her," puts us inside her thoughts. Only she could know that all the men are beautiful to her. After watching her dance and laugh along the beach (the twenty-ninth bather), we return to her thoughts in the lines that follow. We are with her when she splashes with, sees, and loves the young men. We see what she sees: their beards, their long hair, and the little streams that pass all over their bodies. We see her unseen hand passing over the young men's bodies. In the final lines of the poem, we have gone through the looking glass completely. The perspective pulls back to frame the woman among the men, but we are still very much within her fantasy. We see the young men, unawares, as the woman seizes fast to them, puffs and declines, and is soused with their spray, so to speak.

All these details make the passage, to choose a literary critical term of art, hot. Here is innocent lust indeed, made all the more acceptable—for feminists and Marxists, anyway—because the woman does the fantasizing and no money changes hands.

Yet Whitman hoped to do more than just titillate. When you consider what most people in the 1850s, when Whitman wrote the poem, believed about women and sexuality, the passage becomes even more remarkable. Among historians, it is all

the fashion to dismiss the stereotype of what one literary histo-
rian has called "an absurdly proper Victorian America." These
revisionist historians like to point out that beneath the "ice cap
of conventionality" we associate with Victorian America, there
was "a seamy underside," including volumes upon volumes of
pornography and nearly ubiquitous prostitution.[17] And though
the historians have a point, and the seamy underside was real
enough, so too was the ice cap of conventionality.

Crucially, those conventions included the firmly held belief
that women enjoyed sex less than men. Indeed, many believed
women to lack sexual passion entirely. That myth, as Paul R.
Abramson and Steven D. Pinkerton observe, "reached its modern
zenith in the sexually repressed Victorian era of the mid- to late
nineteenth century."[18] In 1857, for example, just two years after
Whitman published the first edition of *Leaves of Grass*, the noted
British physician Dr. William Acton observed in *The Functions
and Disorders of the Reproductive Organs* that "the majority
of women (happily for them) are not very much troubled with
sexual feelings of any kind."[19] "The best mothers, wives, and
managers of households," Acton continued, "know little or noth-
ing of sexual indulgences. Love of home, children, and domestic
duties are the only passion they feel."[20] Women do not love sex,
Acton asserted. They love making a home.

How many people truly believed this myth of the passionless
woman? No one can say, but we can guess how it affected women.
On the one hand, they could think that those who did believe in
the myth of the passionless woman did not know women very
well. On the other hand, they could believe it, and, as a result,
come to deny or denigrate their own sexuality. Either way, the
myth made it difficult if not impossible for women to speak of
their sexual desire.

Consider another Dr. William Acton axiom. "As a general rule," he writes, "a modest woman seldom desires any sexual gratification for herself."[21] Logically, that is like saying A is true because A is true. A sexless woman, Acton asserts, seldom desires sex. Acton may as well have said a brave man fears nothing, or an honest woman seldom tells lies. The statement begs the question, and that would seem to be the point. It makes it impossible for a self-respecting woman to desire sexual gratification. If she *did* desire sexual gratification, she must, by that fact alone, not be a modest woman. That is, she must be an immodest woman. And since few women would want to admit to being immodest, few would acknowledge their desire for sexual gratification. In short, good girls don't. If you do, or want to, you must be a bad girl. And at the time, who among Acton's readers wanted to be a bad girl? Or marry one?

Whitman pierces this circular reasoning. By Acton's logic, a woman could only (and should only) feel shame for her desire. It makes her immodest. Whitman, however, does his best to dispel that shame. He shows us a superficially modest woman—she owns a fine house and wears nice clothes—who nevertheless desires sexual gratification. And he does not just tell us that the woman desires sexual gratification. He shows us, in enough detail to make the fantasy—and the assertion—extraordinarily realistic. (Whitman's own admiration for other men's bodies doubtless helped him to invent the little streams of water that pass over the young men's bodies.)

Here is where the theorizing about shame matters. Aristotle observed that people feel more shame "before those not liable to the same charge."[22] In other words, only those who have not committed the shameful act can look shamefully upon others who have done the shameful thing. For example, I would feel shame if a colleague from work saw me boarding the End Zone shuttle in downtown State College. By contrast, I would feel less shame, or none at all, if I saw that same colleague boarding the shuttle with me. Because my colleague on the shuttle is committing the same sin I am, he is not likely to judge me, and I am not likely to feel shame in front of him. Another colleague, though, who has nothing but contempt for strip clubs, and who presumably has never committed the sin of visiting one, is not liable to the same charge and is therefore free to judge me. Before him, Aristotle asserts, I would feel shame.

Working from this logic, Whitman makes it difficult for anyone to feel shame about her sexual desire because, he insists, everyone, including seemingly modest women, has sexual desires. That is, desire is natural. And if we are all liable to the same charge, if we all feel desire, then no one can—or should—feel shame about it. "I see you," Whitman tells the lady as she hides behind the curtain, not to shame her desires but to acknowledge them.

Whitman offers a similar, though far more charming depiction of natural sexuality in the seventh poem in the "Children of Adam" sequence, which he eventually titled "We Two, How Long We Were Fooled." Because of the bombast of poems like "Song of Myself," people forget that Whitman could also write lovely little poems like this one:

> You and I—what the earth is, we are,
> We two—how long we were fooled!
> Now delicious, transmuted, swiftly we escape, as
>   Nature escapes,
> We are Nature—long have we been absent, but now we return,
> We become plants, leaves, foliage, roots, bark,
> We are bedded in the ground—we are rocks,
> We are oaks—we grow in the openings side by side,
> We browse—we are two among the wild herds, spontaneous
>   as any,

We are two fishes swimming in the sea together,
We are what the locust blossoms are—we drop scent around
   the lanes, mornings and evenings,
We are also the coarse smut of beasts, vegetables,
   minerals.[23]

At some point, Whitman implies, the "We Two" of the poem were fooled into thinking that they transcended nature, were somehow better than it. They realize, however, that, as the opening line says, "what the earth is, we are." That is, they embody nature. Indeed, the transmutation is so complete that they become nature: plants, leaves, foliage, roots, bark, etc.

A lovely poem, but it also illustrates Whitman's fundamental belief that if something occurs in nature, it must have a purpose. It must form part of the plan. Recall that for Whitman, the universe followed certain laws, like conservation of matter or the immutable force of gravity. The existence of those laws implied a rationally ordered universe. Therefore, everything within that rationally ordered universe, including death, must have a reason for being. If Whitman could, against all available evidence, celebrate even something like death as a part of that order, he could, without breaking a sweat, celebrate sex. Indeed, not only did sex belong to the nature of things. For Whitman, it was *the* essential nature of things. It was the fundamental force of the universe. "Urge and urge and urge," Whitman writes in the beginning of "Song of Myself," "always the procreant urge of the world."[24] Because there is something—a universe, planets, people—rather than nothing, Whitman concludes, the universe must be predisposed to creation. It always presses forward. So too nature. It always creates, even when it destroys. Your corpse will make good manure. Your death is another birth, one instance of the always procreant urge.

Men and women, in their lust, share this procreant urge.
Nature created us, and as God did, it created us in its image. We,
too, have an urge to procreate. (At this point, Whitman is think-
ing almost exclusively of heterosexuality.) As in his thoughts
about money, Whitman is attempting to derive an *ought* from
an *is*. Nature is fundamentally creation. Therefore, we ought to
create, which is another way of saying we ought to have sex, and
ought to have the desire to have sex. As a result, Whitman simply
could not accept that sexual desire was something you ought to
apologize for or feel shame about. If anything, like existence itself,
it called for celebration. It called for a poet, and Whitman took
up the mantle.

That is the only way to explain Whitman's enthusiasm about
sex and his commitment to redeeming it from where his culture
had plunged it. "Through me forbidden voices," Whitman writes
in "Song of Myself" not long after the scene with the twenty-
eight young men.

> Voices of sexes and lusts . . . . voices veiled and I remove
>   the veil,
> Voices indecent by me clarified and transfigured.
>
> I do not press my fingers across my mouth,
> I keep as delicate around the bowels as around the head
>   and heart,
> Copulation is no more rank to me than death is.
>
> I believe in the flesh and the appetites,
> Seeing, hearing and feeling are miracles, and each part and tag
>   of me is a miracle.[25]

Voices of sexes and lusts, Whitman writes, are barred, "forbidden," or, just as bad, they are concealed, "veiled," like the twenty-eight-year-old woman who hides behind the blinds of the window as she watches the twenty-eight young men. Explicitly here, but implicitly throughout his poetry, Whitman welcomes these voices back. He returns them to the light of day. But, he tells us, he does more than this. He clarifies and transfigures these supposedly indecent voices. In clarifying them, he frees them from their alleged impurities, just as, in the second meaning of clarify, he makes them easier to understand. He makes it easier for us to hear them. Similarly, by transfiguring these voices, he shapes them into something else, like a sculptor working in clay, and he shapes them, in the second meaning of transfigure, so as to exalt or glorify them.

Moreover, in refusing to press his fingers across his mouth, Whitman admits to sharing these voices of sexes and lusts. Unlike others, he will speak them, for they do not shame him. Quite the opposite. He thinks they glorify him. In short, he makes them decent—more than decent, praiseworthy. Copulation, he boasts, is no more rank to him than death, and he has already told us what a splendid thing death is. Quite simply, he believes in the flesh and the appetites. To do otherwise, to reject the flesh and its appetites, even to doubt them, is to blaspheme nature, which, as we know from poems like "We Two, How Long We Were Fooled," is essentially what we are. You can feel ashamed of your flesh and its appetites, Whitman tells us, but only if you are also willing to be ashamed of the universe and all of existence. You cannot take one without the other.

As the above passages suggest, Whitman took a similar attitude toward the body. It, too, should come out from behind the veil. In the lines that follow those quoted above, Whitman writes:

Divine I am inside and out, and I make holy whatever I touch
    or am touched from;
The scent of these arm-pits is aroma finer than prayer,
This head is more than churches or bibles or creeds.[26]

In asserting the divinity of his body, Whitman is scorning the
conventional Christian belief in the superiority of the soul over
the body. According to this way of thinking, the body is merely
physical, and thus mortal, while the soul partakes of God's light
and is, therefore, both immortal and thus of ultimate conse-
quence. As Paul wrote in his letter to the Galatians: "Live by the
Spirit, I say, and do not gratify the desires of the flesh. For what
the flesh desires is opposed to the Spirit, and what the Spirit
desires is opposed to the flesh."[27] Whitman would have none of
it. Each part and tag of him, including and perhaps especially
the flesh, so far from being fallen or opposed to the Spirit, was a
miracle. If sex forms part of the divine plan, then the instrument,
the body, must share in that divinity as well.

His most famous poem on the subject, "I Sing the Body
Electric," expands on this notion of the divinity of the body.
Midway through the poem, he declares: "The man's body is
sacred, and the woman's body is sacred, it is no matter who."[28]
Therefore the body deserves the respect or reverence accorded
to other holy things. It leads us toward God, not away from
Him.

The "no matter who" in that line is equally crucial. It refers
to what follows in the poem, when Whitman, strangely enough,
stages a slave auction. Since, in his poetry at least, Whitman
views slavery as a moral abhorrence, you would expect him to
protest such an auction. Surprisingly, he does not. Instead, he
offers to "help the auctioneer" since, as he puts it, "the sloven
does not half know his business." His "business" is bodies, and,

Whitman suggests, the auctioneer is not asking nearly enough for the slave bodies he sells. "Gentlemen look on this curious creature," Whitman writes, taking over for the auctioneer, directing attention to the slave on the block.

> Whatever the bids of the bidders they cannot be high enough
>   for him.
> For him the globe lay preparing quintillions of years without
>   one animal or plant,
> For him the revolving cycles truly and steadily rolled.[29]

Whitman's point is that if the value of something is in any way determined by how much time it takes to make it, then a human body, in this case the body of a slave, must be priceless. Think of all the things that must occur for any given person to exist. The universe has to form; within that universe a planet hospitable to life has to cohere; on that planet a spark of life has to catch; and that spark of life, over hundreds of millions of years, has to evolve into mankind, into this singular man on the auction block, with all his exquisite qualities and capacities. A body, then, must be a miracle, though not in the sense of a miracle as something that violates the laws of nature, but a miracle in the sense of something that is a wonderful culmination of the laws of nature. No wonder that, whatever the bids of the bidders, they cannot be high enough.

Whitman asserts that we should no more apologize for our flesh (our bodies) than we should for its appetites (our desires). Characteristically, he disdained perfume. "Houses and rooms," he writes at the outset of "Song of Myself," "are full of perfumes. . . . the shelves are crowded with it."[30] Here, too, Whitman would have none of it. For him, perfumes merely obscure the inherent divinity of the body. As we have seen, he preferred the aroma from his arm-pits, which, he tells us, is finer than prayer. Or, as

he exclaims in "Song of Myself": "Washes and razors for foofoos
. . . . for me freckles and a bristling beard."[31]

Two additional passages can sum up Whitman's attitude
toward the body and sexuality. The first, from "Song of Myself,"
asserts the virtues of the body:

> Welcome is every organ and attribute of me, and of any man
>   hearty and clean,
> Not an inch nor a particle of an inch is vile, and none shall be
>   less familiar than the rest.[32]

The metaphor Whitman chooses matters. Every organ and
attribute of him is "welcome." And no part of his body shall be
less "familiar" than the rest. Whitman is speaking of the body as
one might speak of a guest or a member of the family. His body
is welcome. He will not shut the door on it. He will invite it into
the house. Or, to go with the metaphor behind "familiar," it will
become part of the family.

The second passage comes from "A Woman Waits for Me"
and asserts the virtues of sexuality:

> Without shame the man I like knows and avows the
>   deliciousness of his sex,
> Without shame the woman I like knows and avows hers.[33]

Here, too, Whitman's words matter. If we want Whitman to
like us, and frankly, that is all I want these days, then we must
know and avow the deliciousness of our sex. At first, this phrase
may sound off. Are we to taste our own sex and find it delicious?
Is that even anatomically possible? It seems unlikely. Rather, I
think Whitman means "deliciousness" in the sense of its root
word, *delicate*, which itself derives from *delight*, which was

originally a verb (*delicere*) that meant to allure, entice. In that sense, the deliciousness of our sex refers to its ability to give pleasure (it is delightful) as well as the need for us to give ourselves up to it (it is alluring). Sex, Whitman insists, is pleasurable, and part of its pleasure lies in its capacity to overcome us. "This is the female form," Whitman writes in "I Sing the Body Electric," illustrating his point about the allure of other bodies. "It attracts with fierce undeniable attraction, / I am drawn by its breath as if I were no more than a helpless vapor . . . . all falls aside but myself and it."[34] Moreover, Whitman expects us not simply to know the deliciousness of our sex but to avow it, to declare it openly. It cannot remain a private or unspoken delight. Only by acknowledging it publicly to ourselves and to others can we meet the first and most important requirement of these lines, which is that we must know and avow the deliciousness of our sex "without shame."

Throughout his poetry, Whitman returns again and again to sex, and to bodies, but his point, which he expresses with unusual urgency and clarity, is that something has gone horribly wrong if people feel shame about their body and their sexual desire, which, more than anything else, is part and parcel of the miracle of existence. To put it in terms Freud would recognize, Whitman seeks to make something like sexual desire—and the body that reaps and sows sexual desire—a characteristic of our ego ideal. To feel lust, then, is not to feel that you have abandoned the better angel of your nature, but that you have fulfilled it. You should not feel ashamed of your desires. You should only feel ashamed of your unwillingness to admit them.

It matters, then, that Whitman puts himself in these lines about men and women knowing and avowing the deliciousness of their sex. In Aristotle's view, shame comes from concern with how others view you, or how you believe they will view you.

Shame, Aristotle insists, is found "in the eyes of others." We
fear that when we do something shameful, those we admire or
respect will no longer admire or respect us. In short, they will
no longer like us. Crucially, in this passage and in fact in all of
his writing about sexuality and the body, Whitman offers up
another pair of eyes in which to view ourselves and our bodies.
In his eyes, it is not shameful to welcome every inch or particle
of an inch of your body, as is. Nor is it shameful to know and
avow the deliciousness of your sex. Just the opposite. These are
the men and women whom Whitman likes best. Everyone else
might tut-tut when you climb aboard the shuttle to the strip
club, check sexy books out of the campus library, or fantasize
about twenty-eight young men, but not Whitman. He likes you,
and he likes you best, when you do just these things.

IV.

At first glance, it may seem like Whitman and his war against
shame would have better served an earlier generation and its mal-
aise. After all, when it comes to sexuality, we live in a very differ-
ent world than Whitman did. Say what you will about the sexual
revolution, it changed how most Americans think about sex. By
documenting how Americans actually behaved when it came to
sex, Alfred Kinsey accomplished something like what Whitman
had hoped to achieve. He made sexuality natural. (Kinsey, recall,
began his academic career as a zoologist. To him, we were just
another animal doing what instinct led us to do.) In literature
and film, depictions of sexuality and the body have become so
commonplace and explicit as to make Whitman's efforts seem
quaint, if not downright sentimental. Today, with no more than
an Internet connection or a library card, you can find pages upon

pages of pornography, but you can also find informed, humane discussions of human sexuality.

No revolution ever succeeds completely, however, and the sexual revolution is no different. Take sexual education, for example. Although it may now seem hard to believe, for a brief period, in the 1970s and early 1980s, sex education courses actually informed students about the possibilities, and not just the perils, of sex. That period did not last long. By the end of the 1980s, sex education classes became yet one more casualty in the culture wars between the political right and left. Evangelicals, in particular, came out against any form of sex education that did not condemn premarital sex. For the most part, they won. Today, sex education classes, when they have not been cut from the curriculum altogether, by and large take one of two forms: abstinence-only or abstinence-based. Abstinence-only classes instruct students that, as one journalist summarized, "abstinence until marriage is the only acceptable choice, contraceptives don't work and premarital sex is physically and emotionally harmful." (In *No Second Chances*, a video used in abstinence-only courses, a student asks a school nurse, "What if I want to have sex before I get married?" The nurse replies, "Well, I guess you'll just have to be prepared to die.") In abstinence-based classes, the curriculum emphasizes what embittered sexual educators call "disaster prevention": "Abstinence is usually best, but if you must have sex, here are some ways to protect yourself from pregnancy and disease."[35]

In neither abstinence-only nor abstinence-based classes can anyone consider—or even acknowledge—the pleasure of sex. In contemporary sex ed classes, pleasure itself has become the love that dare not speak its name. In the absence of forthright sex education classes, we mostly let pornography do our teaching, which can provide a quick lesson in the pleasures of sex, I suppose, but which also provides a distorted, occasionally grotesque depiction of it. Not all sex education has to occur in schools, of course, but when, as a culture, we outsource its instruction to parents (at best) and the Internet (at worst), we should not be surprised at the uneven results. If I had my way, every sex ed class would begin with a reading of "Song of Myself." (Then again, if I had my way, every class everywhere, regardless of the subject, would begin with a reading of "Song of Myself.") In that poem, Whitman takes his stand as the poet of sexual pleasure.

To be sure, eyes-wide-shut sex education or not, most of us eventually discover that sex is pleasurable. The danger, then, may not lie in making too little of sexual pleasure, but in making too much of it. Sex, we also eventually learn, occupies only one part of our life. Moreover, as we accumulate responsibilities—jobs, mortgages, children—it is tempting to let it occupy a smaller and smaller part of our life. We may even look back at our younger, give-me-now-libidinous-joys-only selves with a mixture of exasperation and shame. The litany is no doubt familiar. Why in the world did I sleep with that person? Or, more generally, why in the world did I spend—waste—all that time and effort in the pursuit of something as inconsequential as sex? Or, more generally still, what was I thinking? What a relief, we may tell ourselves, to have grown up and put away such childish things.

At that point, when we begin to condescend to our younger or libidinous selves, then Whitman might help us the most. Whitman reminds us that we should not take the pleasure of sex for granted. Nor should we apologize for or regret our past (or present) preoccupation with it. Whitman makes sexuality and the body sublime. Desire is a blessing. Sex, Whitman insists, reveals our place in nature and in the universe. "We are snow, rain, cold, darkness—we are each product and influence of the globe," he writes in "We Too, How Long We Were Fooled."[36] For Whitman, that place is sacred, and so too are our bodies and how they come together with other bodies.

V.

Given his full-throated celebration of the body and its passions, you would think that Whitman would have emerged as an early proponent—or at least apologist—for masturbation. Oddly enough, he did not. Indeed, the subject seems to have made even the unflappable Whitman uncomfortable. To be sure, Whitman never shied away from writing about masturbation. With the exception of Philip Roth or David Foster Wallace, perhaps no American writer has devoted more lines to it than him. Still, unlike his endorsement of sex, which put him at odds with his culture, Whitman never entirely escaped the dread that his contemporaries had about masturbation.

Dread may actually understate things. Panic is more like it. Indeed, masturbation, especially when undertaken by young men, seems to have been the public health crisis of the mid- to late nineteenth century. (Women, who did not desire sexual gratification, as we have learned, were thought to be slightly less of a risk.) Because of what one Swiss physician called its "excessive and unnatural" expenditure of semen, masturbation was thought to deplete the body's energy and expose it to a myriad of ills. Dr. William Acton, he of the keen insights into women's sexuality, argued that masturbation led to impotence, consumption, curvature of the spine, and insanity. In *The Functions and Disorders of the Reproductive Organs*, Acton painted a portrait of the habitual masturbator, who had more in common with a human corpse than a human being:

The frame is stunted and weak, the muscles undeveloped, the eye is sunken and heavy, the complexion is sallow, pasty, or covered with spots of acne, the hands are damp and cold, and the skin moist. The boy shuns the society of others, creeps about alone, joins with repugnance in the amusements of his schoolfellows. He cannot look anyone in the face, and becomes careless in dress and uncleanly in person. His intellect has become sluggish and enfeebled, and if his evil habits are persisted in, he may end in becoming a driveling idiot or a peevish valetudinarian.[37]

The cures for the habitual—or even the potential—masturbator ranged from the relatively benign to the revoltingly horrific. The benign included an especially bland diet, to which we owe such American delicacies as corn flakes and Graham crackers. (John H. Kellogg ran a sanitarium in Battle Creek, Michigan, where he served his patented corn flakes to tamp down masturbatory desires among his patients; and Sylvester Graham was an American health reformer in the 1830s.) The horrific included various efforts at restraining young men while they slept or discouraging them from getting erections. (The details would turn your stomach.)[38]

For his part, Whitman had an uncharacteristically ambivalent attitude toward masturbation. That said, he fills his poetry with language and scenes that evoke it. "The young woman that flushes and flushes," Whitman writes in an 1856 poem,

> and the young man that flushes and flushes,
> The young man that wakes, deep at night, the hot hand seeking
>   to repress what would master him—the strange half-
>   welcome pangs, visions, sweats—the pulse pounding
>   through palms and trembling encircling fingers—the young
>   man all colored, red, ashamed, angry[39]

Nor is this a flush that Whitman claims to stand above. "The like of the same I feel," he admits in the poem; and in "Crossing Brooklyn Ferry," he numbers among his sins that of being "a solitary committer."[40] (Those who campaigned against masturbation referred to it as "the solitary vice.")[41] But that Whitman counts masturbation as one of the things proving he too knew what it was to be evil suggests his misgivings about the practice. In one of the original 1855 poems, Whitman refers to "the sick-gray faces of onanists."[42] In "A Memorandum at a Venture," his defense of *Leaves of Grass* from charges of obscenity, Whitman listed "depletion," a code word for masturbation, as one of the lamentable results of respectable culture remaining silent about sexuality.[43] (No one would warn children of the dangers of masturbation.) Perhaps most revealing, in subsequent versions of "Crossing Brooklyn Ferry," Whitman dropped the phrase "a solitary committer" from the poem. The poet who could welcome every organ and attribute of himself could not, apparently, welcome this.

My point is not to indict Whitman for his ambivalence toward masturbation. No one, not even Whitman, ever fully escapes the assumptions and misperceptions of his or her culture. Rather, I raise the issue because it suggests even Whitman had notions of what constituted proper and improper expressions of sexuality. Whitman worshipped health, and he worshipped young men and women, who, he believed, would ultimately determine the fate of the United States. Convinced that masturbation harmed bodies, especially the bodies of the young, Whitman, understandably, I think, acknowledged the temptations and pleasures of masturbation but could not endorse it as he did other forms of sexuality.

Masturbation, of course, does not deplete your precious bodily energy, nor will it harm the fate of these United States. Today, we know better. (Or I would like to think so. As late as 1994, Bill Clinton fired his Surgeon General, Joycelyn Elders, after she asserted, at a United Nations conference on AIDS, that masturbation "is part of human sexuality, and it's a part of something that perhaps should be taught.")[44] Still, Whitman's ambivalence toward masturbation reminds us that he did not believe that anything goes. As much as Whitman can seem to have in common with the radicals who led the charge of the sexual revolution, he differs from them as well. For example, he is no Fritz Perls, the German-born psychiatrist and founder of Gestalt therapy who developed a cult following in the United States in the 1960s for preaching, effectively, hedonism and unfettered sexual expression. "I do my thing and you do your thing," his Gestalt prayer began. "I am not in this world to live up to your expectations," it continued, "And you are not in this world to live up to mine."[45]

Perls and his acolytes illustrate what happens when the transcendence of shame about sexuality passes into the depths of shamelessness. Shame may represent one source of malaise about sexuality, but shamelessness does, too. If shame, as Aristotle believed, comes from "the eyes of others," shamelessness comes from a systematic indifference to what others think of our behavior. (Recall the Gestalt prayer.) When we pass into the realm of shamelessness, we come to believe that sex is the most gratifying part of human existence. Worse, we may come to imagine that other people exist only to gratify our sexual desires. In short, we say, our bodies are sacred, and everyone else's must pay homage to it. In Freudian terms, shamelessness makes for its own sort of narcissism. We love our selves too much. We can do no wrong. Indeed, in *The Culture of Narcissism*, Christopher Lasch had Perls and other post-Freudian therapists in mind when he wrote of those "for whom mental health means the overthrow of inhibitions and the immediate gratification of every impulse."[46]

Nor have we completely left the "me" decade and its culture of narcissism behind. When the Monica Lewinsky scandal broke, Bill Clinton reportedly called Dick Morris, his political consultant, and confessed, "Ever since I got here to the White House I've had to shut my body down, sexually I mean, but I screwed up with this girl. I didn't do what they said I did, but I may have done so much that I can't prove my innocence."[47] On the one hand, you can pity Clinton for feeling as if he had to shut down his body sexually. On the other hand, the way he started it up again—what he *did* do with Lewinsky—is sickening, not because of the sex but because of the narcissism. It took Bill Clinton about four months, and six bouts of oral sex, before he and Monica Lewinsky had what "The Starr Report" called their "first lengthy and personal conversation."[48] Prior to that, Clinton treated Lewinsky like a car and a pair of jumper cables, a way to get his dead battery of a body running again. Many of their liaisons occurred while Clinton took phone calls.[49]

Clinton, who later gave Lewinsky a copy of Whitman's *Leaves of Grass*, on the same day that she wore the infamous blue dress, had either read Whitman too closely or not closely enough.[50] Too closely because, alas, with his talk of "libidinous joys only," Whitman can seem to license this kind of narcissism and singular concern with your body, with whether it is shut down sexually or up and running, churning through others' bodies.

But reading these poems alone misses Whitman's point, which is what I mean when I say Clinton may not have read Whitman closely enough. Yes, we should know and avow the deliciousness of our sex, Whitman insists, but he is almost as insistent that this does not mean we should let it turn others' bodies to our uses, as Clinton arguably did with Lewinsky's. Indeed, one of the remarkable things about Whitman's poems about sex and the body is how seldom his point is gratification alone and how often his point is about how sex joins people at the hips, how it brings them together. (This may further explain Whitman's anxiety about masturbation, the "solitary" vice.) The principal problem of the twenty-eight-year-old woman who fantasizes about the twenty-eight young men is that she is lonely. The twenty-eight young men relieve that loneliness. The title of Whitman's moving little poem is not "I Was Fooled" but "We Two, How Long We Were Fooled." Whitman vows to remove the veil from voices of sexes and lusts not only because he wants to dispel the air of indecency around them, but also because he wants to bring those voices back into the social fold. They too shall be welcome. And even when Whitman is at his most lustful, when he demands "libidinous joys only," he does so because the pursuit of those joys will bring him closer to his companions. "O you shunned persons!" he writes, "I will not shun you, / I come forthwith in your midst."

I do not mean, and I do not think Whitman means, that sex always has to be about other people, that you have to marry and grow old with whomever you sleep with, or that you should masturbate in public to make it less of a solitary vice. Only that if more often than not your desires go through others only to lead back to yourself, to your own fantasies and needs, you might be doing it wrong. Similarly, if more often than not you find yourself merely fulfilling the desires and fantasies of others, you might also be doing it wrong. Sex should relieve our loneliness, not add to it. Shame adds to it when we come to believe that our desires differentiate us from everyone else, and shamelessness adds to it when we treat our body and our self as the only body and self that matters. Both shame and shamelessness leave us more alone than when we started. But sex, which can drive us apart, can join us together, too, which seems to be Whitman's parting wisdom. Sex can dispel our sense of exile, from each other, from nature, from the universe itself.

In the end, that may be what is wrong with strip clubs. Not that (or only that) they exploit women, or flatter the worst impulses in men, but that at the end of the night, almost everyone goes home alone. They are merely a shabby substitute for what we really ought to be doing.

Was Walt Whitman Gay?

S everal years ago, Ph.D. in hand, I went looking for a job as an English professor. Usually, hundreds of candidates apply for a job, ten are given initial interviews, and then three are invited to campus. On campus, you give a talk based on your research to the rest of the department or, at schools where teaching matters more than research, you teach a class while a few members of the department look on. For a job at a public university in the South, I was asked to teach a class on Walt Whitman's "Song of Myself." What luck, I thought. But after walking students through the ins and outs of the opening sections of the poem—how Whitman joins all the things (body and soul, life and death, north and south, slave and slave master) his culture did its best to keep apart—I paused to ask if anyone had any questions. A young woman boldly raised her hand and asked, "Was Whitman gay?"

From her tone, I guessed that she liked Whitman, but if the answer to her question was yes, she might have to reconsider. In retrospect, I should have just answered yes and been done with it. But instead I told her the truth, which is that a lot of circumstantial evidence suggests that yes, Whitman was gay, but he did not think of himself as such. To add to the confusion, the question itself may not make sense. In the nineteenth century, as I explain below, no one was, strictly speaking, gay.

It did not come up that day, but how we answer this question matters because Whitman thinks about democracy in startlingly personal terms, and if you think that his poems about manly love, comrades, and democracy are really just poems about his homosexuality, then the political dimensions of the poems, which I explore in the next chapter, will mean far less than their sexual ones—and that would be a shame, I think, because we desperately need to hear what Whitman has to say about politics.

I.

On the surface, the poems Whitman wrote for the 1860 edition of *Leaves of Grass*, which he grouped under the heading "Calamus," would seem to settle the question of whether he was gay or not. In the very first poem of the sequence, Whitman resolves "to tell the secret of [his] nights and days" and "to sing no songs to-day but those of manly attachment," and throughout the forty-five poems that make up the sequence, he keeps his word.[1] The poems, as one critic notes, have "come to be celebrated as a homosexual manifesto."[2]

The calamus plant, with flowering spike

Indeed, the title of the sequence itself might put a stop to further inquiry. The flowering spike that grows from the calamus plant looks—there is no other way to put it—like an erect penis.

In addition to their suggestive title, the poems seem straightforwardly gay. The sequence includes stunning love poems like this one:

When I heard at the close of the day how my name had been
    received with plaudits in the capitol, still it was not a happy
    night for me that followed;
And else, when I caroused, or when my plans were
    accomplished, still I was not happy;
But the day when I rose at dawn from the bed of perfect health,
    refreshed, singing, inhaling the ripe breath of autumn,
When I saw the full moon in the west grow pale and disappear
    in the morning light,
When I wandered alone over the beach, and, undressing,
    bathed, laughing with the cool waters, and saw the sun rise,
And when I thought how my dear friend, my lover, was on his
    way coming, O then I was happy;
O then each breath tasted sweeter—and all that day my food
    nourished me more—And the beautiful day passed well,
And the next came with equal joy—And with the next, at
    evening, came my friend;
And that night, while all was still, I heard the waters roll slowly
    continually up the shores,
I heard the hissing rustle of the liquid and sands, as directed to
    me, whispering, to congratulate me,
For the one I love most lay sleeping by me under the same
    cover in the cool night,
In the stillness, in the autumn moonbeams, his face was
    inclined toward me,

And his arm lay lightly around my breast—And that night I
 was happy.[3]

Notice how the clauses pile up only to end in short, declarative statements: "O then I was happy," or later, "And that night I was happy." It is a masterpiece. Whitman turns a theme already exhausted in his own day—only the love of another truly satisfies—into a moving, quiet, and above all tender poem.

In addition to love poems, "Calamus" also includes forsaken-love poems like this one:

Hours continuing long, sore and heavy-hearted,
Hours of the dusk, when I withdraw to a lonesome and
 unfrequented spot, seating myself, leaning my face
 in my hands;
Hours sleepless, deep in the night, when I go forth, speeding
 swiftly the country roads, or through the city streets, or
 pacing miles and miles, stifling plaintive cries;
Hours discouraged, distracted—for the one I cannot content
 myself without, soon I saw him content himself
 without me;
Hours when I am forgotten (O weeks and months are passing,
 but I believe I am never to forget!)
Sullen and suffering hours! (I am ashamed—but it is useless—I
 am what I am);
Hours of my torment—I wonder if other men ever have the l
 like, out of like feelings?
Is there even one other like me—distracted—his friend, his
 lover, lost to him?
Is he too as I am now? Does he still rise in the morning,
 dejected, thinking who is lost to him? and at night, awaking,
 think who is lost?

> Does he too harbor his friendship silent and endless? harbor
>   his anguish and passion?
> Does some stray reminder, or the casual mention of a name,
>   bring the fit back upon him, taciturn and deprest?
> Does he see himself reflected in me? In these hours, does he
>   see the face of his hours reflected?[4]

Unlike "When I Heard at the Close of Day," this poem is a moving testament to loneliness and the various forms it takes. There is the loneliness that comes from being forgotten by a lover, and then the loneliness of wondering whether other men react so passionately to being forgotten by their lovers. In his shifting misery, all the speaker wants is company.

The wonderful thing about both poems, I believe, is that Whitman does not assume that love for another man is something he must defend or treat as a peculiarity. Instead, he takes such relationships as a given and then explores the emotions that result: anticipation, joy, despair, loneliness. In other words, there is nothing the least bit unnatural about these relationships. As in the first poem, nature itself—the beach and the sea—seem to congratulate Whitman on finally uniting with his lover.

At the same time, as the second of these two poems suggests, Whitman occasionally hints that he has something to feel ashamed of, something to hide, which, to those reading today, looks like the torment of someone neither fully in nor fully out of the closet. "I am ashamed," he tells us in "Hours Continuing Long," and in another poem Whitman writes:

> Who is now reading this?
> . . . .
>   . . . may-be one who is puzzled at me.
> As if I were not puzzled at myself.

Or as if I never deride myself! (O conscience-struck!
    O self-convicted!)
Or as if I do not secretly love strangers! (O tenderly, a long
    time, and never avow it);
Or as if I did not see, perfectly well, interior in myself, the stuff
    of wrong-doing,
Or as if it could cease transpiring from me until it must cease.[5]

On the one hand, the speaker recognizes "the stuff of wrong-doing" in him. On the other hand, he understands that he can do nothing about it. It has a life of its own. "I am what I am," he declares with a mixture of pride and resignation in "Hours Continuing Long."[6]

Not for nothing, then, have readers wanted to claim Whitman as gay. He gives voice not only to the ordinariness of extraordinary love for another person of the same sex, including its potential disappointment, but also to the sense of shame, despair, and fear that has often accompanied such love.

For all of that, though, perhaps the best evidence for Whitman's anxious homosexuality comes in the poems he changed or cut for different editions of his book. When Whitman published another edition of *Leaves of Grass* in 1867, for example, he deleted two of the poems from the 1860 edition that I quote above ("Hours Continuing Long" and "Who Is Now Reading This?"). Both poems would seem to have revealed more than Whitman felt comfortable revealing.

Moreover, in the 1920s, one of Whitman's first biographers, Emory Halloway, discovered that one of the poems, "Once I Passed Through a Populous City," written for the "Children of Adam" sequence of poems, which, if you'll remember from chapter 3, celebrates the love between men and women, had in the original manuscript described Whitman's love for a man and not a woman. Whitman simply changed the pronouns. The discovery seems to have undone its discoverer, Holloway. Afterward, he set out to prove Whitman's heterosexuality by tracking down one of the six children Whitman claimed—falsely—to have fathered. (More on these invented children below.)[7]

Similarly, in the 1950s, another Whitman scholar, Fredson Bowers, discovered that Whitman originally conceived of twelve of the "Calamus" poems as a single cluster of poems, which he titled, after one of the poems, "Live Oak, with Moss." Reconstructed, the sequence vividly narrates a love affair with a man. (The poem quoted above, "When I Heard at the Close of Day," was the third poem in the sequence. "Hours Continuing Long," also quoted above, was the eighth.) Yet when Whitman assembled the "Calamus" poems for the 1860 edition of *Leaves of Grass*, he scrambled the "Live Oak, with Moss" sequence, effectively destroying the narrative, again, critics argue, because it would have revealed too much.[8]

For many readers, these changes and deletions look like censorship, whether because Whitman felt ashamed of his homosexuality or, more likely, because he understood what the public would and would not tolerate when it came to homosexuality. Even Whitman knew there were some lines you could not cross.

In any case, all of this evidence—plus some that I have not cited, like the homoerotic elements of other poems, Whitman's habit of attaching himself to young working-class men, and some second- and third-hand testimony—seems to add up to one conclusion: Whitman was gay, and "Calamus," including its emendations and deletions, tells the story. Moreover, or so the argument sometimes goes, anyone who says otherwise must be in the grips of homosexual panic or want to "save" Whitman from homosexuality.

II.

To tell the truth, I wish the story was that simple. As this book makes clear on virtually each of its pages, I am a died-in-the-wool liberal, in love with tolerance as much as the next liberal, and it would doubtless help the cause of tolerance if someone as saintly as Whitman was definitively gay. If, as numerous scholars have pointed out, the source of homophobia is disgust, it is very hard to be disgusted by Whitman. As the poems quoted above attest, he makes love for another person of the same sex seem deeply human, as sweet and turbulent as any other love. Moreover, think what good it would do young men and women suffering from harassment and self-hatred to read an unapologetically—or mostly so—gay poet like Whitman.

But the truth is that if you tug at them even a little, each of the arguments for Whitman's homosexuality begins to unravel. That does not mean Whitman was not gay, but it does make it a much more difficult question to answer.

Take the title of the sequence, "Calamus." Yes, the plant, when it flowers, looks rather obviously phallic, but Whitman seems to have chosen the plant as his title for other reasons. In 1867, the critic William Rossetti planned to bring out the first edition of Whitman's poems for British readers. On Rossetti's behalf, Moncure Conway, an American minister and Whitman acquaintance living in London, wrote the poet with several questions, including "What is Calamus?" "I could not tell him [Rossetti], satisfactorily," Conway wrote, "either the exact thing you meant or its metaphorical meaning to you."[9] In his return letter, Whitman explained:

> "Calamus" is a common word here; it is the very large and aro-
> matic grass, or root, spears three feet high—often called "sweet

flag"—grows all over the Northern and Middle States—(see Webster's Large Dictionary—Calamus—definition 2). The recherché or ethereal sense, as used in my book, arises probably from it, Calamus presenting the biggest and hardiest kind of spears of grass, and from its fresh, aromatic, pungent bouquet.[10]

Although the syntax is confusing, the "it" from which Whitman draws his "recherché or ethereal sense" is that calamus "grows all over the Northern and Middle States." In other words, Whitman liked the calamus plant for the same reason he liked other species of grass. Namely, it sprouted everywhere, and in doing so it joined people together. As he put it in "Song of Myself," he guessed that grass

> is a uniform hieroglyphic
> And it means, Sprouting alike in broad zones and
> narrow zones,
> Growing among black folks as among white,
> Kanuck, Tuckahoe, Congressman, Cuff, I give them the same,
> I receive them the same.[11]

"Kanuck" refers to a French Canadian; "Tuckahoe," in a roundabout way, to Virginians; and "Cuff" was a slang term for African Americans. As these and other passages make clear, grass, including calamus, appealed to Whitman for its democratic qualities. Like Whitman, it did not distinguish between high and low. And as Whitman aspired to, it grew everywhere, among everyone. If calamus had any extra appeal, it was that it grew in out-of-the-way places, "away from the clank of the world," as he put it in the first poem in the "Calamus" sequence.[12] It thus grew in the marginal places where, Whitman believed, "manly attachment"—and what he means by that remains unclear—could also flower, far from the "pleasures, profits, conformities" of everyday life.[13] That sense of calamus as a particularly hearty, egalitarian, and conjoining grass does not undo its flowering phallus, of course, and whatever meaning Whitman attached to it, but that part of the plant does not seem to have preoccupied him.

Then there is the matter of Whitman's revisions and deletions. True, poems like "Hours Continuing Long" and "Who Is Now Reading This?" disappeared from subsequent editions. But poems like "When I Heard at the Close of Day"—including that very poem—very much remained. What's more, the sequence as a whole still begins with Whitman "resolved to sing no songs to-day but those of manly attachment," and the sequence still has Whitman "burning for his love whom I love," still has Whitman permitting "a candidate for my affection" to "put your lips upon mine," and still has Whitman telling a passing stranger that "you do not know how longingly I look upon you."[14] In other words, if Whitman hoped by scattering the poems to conceal the more explicit statements of his homosexuality, to stuff the more revealing lines (and himself) back in the closet, he did an extraordinarily bad job of it.

But Whitman does not seem to have wielded the editor's pen with those concerns in mind. Rather, in deciding which poems to cut, he appears to have targeted the gloomier poems. In the first poem in the "Calamus" sequence, Whitman vows to "celebrate the need of comrades." If so, then Whitman may have realized that poems of despair and self-doubt like "Hours Continuing Long" and "Who Is Now Reading This?" did not fit the mood. After one less than celebratory poem in the sequence, for instance, Whitman vows early in the following poem that "I must change the strain—these are not to be pensive leaves, but leaves of joy."[15] In short, Whitman likely dropped poems not because they revealed too much, but because he did not like what they revealed, namely despair.

As for why Whitman scattered throughout the "Calamus" sequence the highly personal series of poems that made up "Live Oak, with Moss," we may never know. (In fact, "Live Oak, with Moss" is not as exclusively personal as some critics have suggested.) One thing is clear, though, which is that as the "Calamus" sequence appears in the 1860 and subsequent editions, the "Live Oak, with Moss" sequence, had it appeared intact, would have seemed very much out of place. In the first poem, Whitman confides that he will tell us "the secrets of his nights and days," but he also says that he will do so in order "to celebrate the need of comrades." In other words, for Whitman, the purpose of the "Calamus" poems was not (or not principally) to narrate an affair of his personal life but to make the case, poetically, for the need of comrades. All told, Whitman wrote forty-five poems for the "Calamus" sequence. Nearly all of these are what we would call personal poems—they are spoken in the first person, anyway—but many of them also have what we would call a rhetorical, even public purpose. As he writes in one poem, he hopes to "establish . . . in every city of These States . . . the institution of the dear love of comrades."[16] It would thus look strange—and subvert his stated purpose for the poems—to narrate the rise and fall of a single love affair. Whitman is not interested in *a* love affair, but in propagating—like grass—as many love affairs as possible. For Whitman, the personal is political. The original sequence of poems—and the original affair—may have inspired the "Calamus" poems, and you may prefer "Live Oak, with Moss" over "Calamus" as a sequence of poems. (I go back and forth.) But Whitman had reasons enough besides shame or secrecy to break up the original sequence. And that makes sense when you think about it, because Whitman never seems to have felt ashamed or secretive about anything he had published, including the "Calamus" poems.

Perhaps the oddest part of this whole story, though, is how Whitman's contemporary readers reacted to the "Calamus" poems. True, some reviewers—and many readers—thought that Whitman was obscene, but he got that reputation not for the "Calamus" poems but for the "Children of Adam" poems, the ones that celebrated the love between men and women. Whitman, a London reviewer wrote of the 1860 edition, is "one of the most indecent writers who ever raked out filth into sentences." "Do American ladies read Mr. Whitman?" the reviewer asked incredulously.[17] And in 1881, when the district attorney of Boston declared the book obscene, it was those poems—specifically, "A Woman Waits for Me" and "Ode to a Common Prostitute"—that offended him.[18] By contrast, no one, neither readers nor reviewers nor district attorneys, seems to have batted an eye about the "Calamus" poems.

That should give us pause. If in writing "Calamus" Whitman is supposed to have written a homosexual manifesto, then why weren't people shocked? He was not exactly subtle. And if no one was shocked, why did he supposedly revise his poems as though they were? For proponents of a gay Whitman, or, more narrowly, "Calamus" as gay poetry, these questions remain the greatest unsolved mysteries.[19]

III.

But really it is no mystery at all. As many critics have pointed out, Whitman's poems of manly love fit perfectly well into the nineteenth-century cult of romantic friendship. As historians have now rather fully documented, men (and women) in the

nineteenth century often developed passionate—even inti-
mate—friendships with others of the same sex.[20] To observers
then and now, these friendships looked like a sort of marriage,
probably without the sex but decidedly not without the intense
affection. To judge from their diaries and letters, young men
in these romantic friendships addressed each other in flowery
terms of endearment, waxed over their ardent feelings for each
other, and often expressed a hope that they might share a life
together. They make Whitman's similar effusions seem down-
right ordinary.

From our perspective, the strangest thing about these roman-
tic friendships is how much physical affection they allowed. It
is not just that friends shared a bed. (In the nineteenth century,
sharing a bed with another person of the same gender, whether
a sibling, friend, or even stranger—recall Ishmael and Queequeg
at the outset of *Moby Dick*—was part of daily life.) Rather, it was
what happened in those shared beds that seems so bizarre. In
July of 1851, for example, two young engineers, James Blake
and Wyck Vanderhoef, who shared a room (and a bed), departed
for their family homes. After their separation, in his diary James
Blake described their last night together:

> We retired early, but long was the time before our eyes were
> closed in slumber, for this was the last night we shall be together
> for the present, and our hearts were full of that true friendship
> which could not find utterance by words, we laid our heads
> upon each other's bosom and wept, it may be unmanly to weep,
> but I care not, the spirit was touched.[21]

In the late 1830s, another diarist, Albert Dodd, wrote of his
college roommate, Anthony Halsey, "Often too he shared my
pillow—or I his, and then how sweet to sleep with him, to hold

his beloved form in my embrace, to have his arms about my neck, to imprint upon his face sweet kisses!"[22]

To our eyes, this intimacy will seem peculiar. However, it seems not to have bothered—far from it—those in bed. As noted by E. Anthony Rotundo, the historian who has looked most closely at these diaries, Dodd "described their erotic encounter without a hint of self-censure or a word of apology."[23] Of Blake's description of his last night with Vanderhoef, Rotundo observes that "apparently crying violated the norms of manliness more than the exchange of affectionate physical gestures with another man."[24]

How could men get away with such intimacy? One theory argues that in the nineteenth century, intimate friends, even those who shared a pillow or imprinted upon each other sweet kisses, did not have to fear being mistaken for homosexuals, and this made affection between men (and women) less fraught. Indeed, as a college student somewhere is no doubt learning this very moment, you could not be a homosexual in the nineteenth century. The term—the concept—did not exist. That does not mean that men did not have sex with each other. (Even Whitman refers to the "he-prostitutes.") But it does mean that men could kiss each other in bed or in the streets without worrying that their affection would be viewed as a symptom of some ingrained disease like homosexuality. "In the Victorian language of touch," Rotundo writes, "a kiss or an embrace was a gesture of strong affection at least as much as it was an act of sexual expression."[25]

Perhaps here is the place to note, then, that when Whitman speaks of "my dear friend, my lover," as he does in "When I Heard at the Close of Day," the terms are synonyms. At the time, *lover* simply meant someone you loved, not someone you made love to, and as such, men felt far less anxiety about expressing love for their male friends or calling their friends their lovers. In his essay on friendship, for example, Ralph Waldo Emerson writes, "High thanks I owe you, excellent lovers, who carry out the world for me to new and noble depths."[26] It was Emerson, you will recall, who in 1860 tried to talk Whitman out of publishing the "Children of Adam" sequence. He said nothing, apparently, about the "Calamus" poems, perhaps because while at Harvard he too had a strange though intense attraction to another fellow student.[27]

None of this, of course, means that the young men in these relationships did not have sex. But at the same time nothing suggests they did have sex, either. Rotundo observes, "Intimate friends were not engaging in genital sexuality or they did not feel safe in writing about it"; and the former seems more likely than the latter.[28] The curious thing about such professions of romantic friendship (again, only curious from our perspective) is that often enough they existed alongside professions of conventional heterosexual love. At the time James Blake wept over his separation from his friend, for example, his friend was engaged to be married. The diary in which Albert Dodd described his nights with Anthony Halsey also contains rapturous entries—including love poems—about young women named Julia and Elizabeth. Indeed, while sharing a bed, men seemed to talk about women as much as anything else.[29]

Again, none of this rules out the possibility that men in these relationships had sex with each other. Nothing says you can't have sex with people of both genders. Yet sex does not seem to have been the characteristic feature of these relationships. More to the point, the cult of romantic friendship make Whitman's professions of manly love not before their time but very much of it.

IV.

Perhaps the most useful context for Whitman's poems of manly love, however, comes from the pseudoscience of phrenology, which Whitman swallowed hook, line, and sinker. In phrenology, parts of the brain (and their relative size) supposedly corresponded to various character traits. Moreover, since the skull was thought to match the shape of the brain beneath it, your skull was also thought to reveal the contours of your character. Is the base of your skull larger than usual? That means you have an unusually large capacity for sexual and connubial love. Does the back of your skull bone protrude? That means you are especially philoprogenitive. (You love your children.) Do the areas above and to the left and right of it protrude more than usual? Then you are particularly adhesive, which means, as Whitman's favorite phrenologists, Orson and Lorenzo Fowler, wrote, you love "friends with tenderness" and will "sacrifice almost anything for their sake."[30] Elsewhere, Orson Fowler would explain that those with large adhesiveness "instinctively recognize it in each other; soon become mutually and strongly attached; desire to cling to the objects of their love; take more delight in the exercise of their friendship than in anything else."[31]

In the diagram to the right, which the Fowlers included in their 1855 book, *The Illustrated Self-Instructor in Phrenology and Physiology*, amativeness (sexual and connubial love) is near but distinct from adhesiveness (friendship, sociability). (Adhesiveness is illustrated by two sisters embracing.) As with any other trait one could be more or less amative or adhesive, and the point beyond that is that one could be both amative and adhesive. Amativeness tracked connubial love, while adhesiveness meant friendship, sociability. In 1849, Whitman had his skull examined by Lorenzo Fowler. He scored highly in, among other

132 OUTLINES OF PHRENOLOGY.

Fig. 165.—Symbolical Head.

Explanation.—No. 1. Amativeness is represented by Cupid, with his bow and arrow. No. 3. Adhesiveness, by two sisters embracing. No. 6. Combativeness—perverted—by two boys contending. No. 9. Acquisitiveness, a miser counting his gold. No. 10. Secretiveness, by a cat watching for a mouse. B. Sublimity, Niagara Falls. 24. Individuality, a boy with a telescope. 31. Locality, by a traveler consulting a guide-board. 36. Causality, Newton studying the laws of gravity by the falling of an apple. 18. Veneration, devotion, and deference, respect, and prayer. 19 Benevolence, the Good Samaritan bestowing charity. No. 17. Spirituality, Moses, on Mount Sinai, receiving the tables from Heaven on which were engraved the Ten Commandments. 16. Hope, the anchor, and a ship at sea. 15. Conscientiousness, Justice, with the scales in one hand and the sword in the other, and so forth. Each organ is represented by a symbol, which in some cases may show the appropriate, and in others the perverted action. The latter is shown in case of the miser, the glutton, and the fighting boys. It is used as a means of indicating both the location of the organs and to show their natural action as frequently exhibited in life.

Note.—The reader will observe here the natural grouping of the organs. Consider, for instance, the relations so admirably indicated in the arrangement in contiguity of Amativeness, Parental Love, Friendship, and Inhabitiveness; or of Alimentiveness, Acquisitiveness, Secretiveness, Destructiveness, and Combativeness. So Individuality, Form, Size, Weight, Color, Order, and the rest of the Perceptive organs, indicate by their locations their common matter-of-fact tendencies.

The phrenological skull

categories, both amativeness and adhesiveness. He received a 6 out of possible 7 in both categories.[32] Indeed, the phrenological chart may illustrate why diarists like James Blake could speak of their love for their friend and their love for their fiancée on virtually the same page. Such loves involved related but distinct traits. In the "Calamus" poems, Whitman also says as much. Here is the thirty-eighth poem:

> Primeval my love for the woman I love,
> O bride! O wife! more resistless, more endearing than I can
>   tell, the thought of you!
> Then separate, as disembodied, the purest born,
> The ethereal, the last athletic reality, my consolation,
> I ascend—I float in the regions of your love, O man,
> O sharer of my roving life.[33]

As the poem suggests, love for women could jauntily exist alongside love of men. Each love met different needs and expressed different capacities. They seem to have occurred on different planes of reality. In any case, one did not cancel out the other, just as the "Children of Adam" sequence could happily exist alongside the "Calamus" sequence in the 1860 edition and subsequent editions of *Leaves of Grass*.

Throughout his life, Whitman seems to have thought of manly love in phrenological terms. (He seems to have thought of an astonishing number of things in phrenological terms.) In "Proto-Leaf," the new poem he composed to lead off the 1860 edition of *Leaves of Grass*, he writes:

> O to level occupations and the sexes! O to bring all to common
>   ground! O adhesiveness!

> O the pensive aching to be together—you know not why, and I
> know not why.[34]

In the sixth Calamus poem, he writes, "O adhesiveness! O pulse of my life!" And in the final poem of the 1860 edition, "So long!" he declares:

> I announce adhesiveness—I say it shall be limitless,
> unloosened,
> I say you shall yet find the friend you was looking for.[35]

Perhaps the most revealing statement, however, comes in *Democratic Vistas*. There, Whitman says in a footnote:

> It is to the development, identification, and general prevalence of that fervid comradeship, (the adhesive love, at least rivaling the amative love hitherto possessing imaginative literature, if not going beyond it,) that I look for the counterbalance and offset of our materialistic and vulgar American democracy, and for the spiritualization thereof. Many will say it is a dream, and will not follow my inferences: but I confidently expect a time when there will be seen, running like a half-hid warp through all the myriad audible and visible worldly interests of America, threads of manly friendship, fond and loving, pure and sweet, strong and life-long, carried to degrees hitherto unknown—not only giving tone to individual character, and making it unprecedently emotional, muscular, heroic, and refined, but having the deepest relations to general politics. I say democracy infers such loving comradeship, as its most inevitable twin or counterpart, without which it will be incomplete, in vain, and incapable of perpetuating itself.[36]

In the next chapter, I take up the political implications of the kind of comradeship Whitman describes here and in "Calamus," but for now what matters is how he speaks of it. Or rather, the many ways he speaks of it: comradeship, adhesive love, manly friendship, loving comradeship. For Whitman, these are synonyms. Thus when he writes, as he does in the first "Calamus" poem, that he intends to "celebrate the need of comrades," he seems to have something very specific in mind. It involves many things (emotions, affection, politics), but it does not seem to have involved sex.

In that case, phrenology and the cult of romantic friendship may explain why "Calamus" did not raise eyebrows. Readers knew what Whitman was talking about, and they knew he was not talking about connubial love between men. To all but a few, that sort of love would have been unthinkable. Instead, he was talking about romantic friendships, and these friendships were common enough not to outrage decency but also rare—and private—enough to require public and poetic celebrants. Or so Whitman thought. Hence his aside in the passage above from *Democratic Vistas*. Thus far, he argues, imaginative literature had focused almost exclusively on amative love, to the neglect of the equally powerful adhesive love. Or, as Whitman wrote in an 1856 open letter to Ralph Waldo Emerson, "As to manly friendship, everywhere observed in The States, there is not the first breath of it to be observed in print."[37] With the "Calamus" sequence, Whitman would change all that.

V.

So was Whitman gay? Or, more narrowly, are the "Calamus" poems gay poems?

The second question is easier to answer than the first. Whitman certainly did not think the poems indicated he was gay, and at the very least we need to hear him out. As we have seen, Whitman thought of "Calamus" in phrenological terms of adhesiveness, and he thought of adhesiveness in its private *and* political dimensions. In the "Preface" to the 1876 reprint of *Leaves of Grass*, for example, Whitman discussed "the special meaning of the 'Calamus' cluster":

> Important as they are in my purpose as emotional expressions for humanity, the special meaning of the "Calamus" cluster of "Leaves of Grass," (and more or less running throughout the book, and cropping out in "Drum Taps,") mainly resides in its political significance. In my opinion, it is by a fervent, accepted development of comradeship, the beautiful and sane affection of man for man, latent in all the young fellows, north and south, east and west—it is by this, I say, and by what goes directly and indirectly along with it, that the United States of the future, (I cannot too often repeat,) are to be most effectually welded together, intercalated, anneal'd into a living union.[38]

Nor does Whitman seem to have invented this explanation of the special meaning of the "Calamus" cluster in order to distract readers from its (or his) homoeroticism. The political significance existed from the start. How else can we explain the fifth poem in the "Calamus" sequence? "States!" Whitman declares, which is not a promising beginning for a poem about sex:

> Were you looking to be held together by the lawyers?
> By an agreement on a paper? Or by arms?

Away!
I arrive, bringing these, beyond all the forces of courts
    and arms,
These! to hold you together as firmly as the earth itself is
    held together.

The "these" Whitman brings refers to the "Calamus" poems, by which, he writes in the conclusion of the poem:

I will make the continent indissoluble,
I will make the most splendid race the sun ever yet
    shone upon,
I will make divine magnetic lands.

I will plant companionship thick as trees along all the rivers of
    America, and along the shores of the great lakes, and all
    over the prairies,
I will make inseparable cities, with their arms about each
    other's necks.[39]

Notice the plant metaphor in the next to last line. On the eve of the Civil War, with the nation, as Lincoln put it, a house divided against itself, Whitman would plant companionship "thick as trees" among the states. He would unite a divided nation. The last line of the poem makes his point. Cities will become like young men with their arms about each other's necks when real young men, perhaps having read *Leaves of Grass*, would be inspired to throw their arms around each other's necks. The nation would come together when its young men came together in loving comradeship.

All of which is to say, whatever we might infer about the sexual dimensions of the poems or the sexuality of the poet, we ought to acknowledge, as Whitman insisted again and again, their political dimensions.

That, anyway, is what Whitman declared in a famous letter that sheds light on both the "Calamus" poems and the question of his sexuality. In 1872, the British poet, literary critic, and biographer John Addington Symonds wrote Whitman an enthusiastic letter asking—begging—for more information about the "Calamus" poems. At the time, Symonds was struggling with how to understand his own attraction to men, and over the course of the next twenty years he would pioneer the study of homosexuality. "I have pored for continuous hours over the pages of Calamus (as I used to pore over the pages of Plato)," Symonds wrote Whitman, "longing to hear you speak, burning for a revelation of your more developed meaning, panting to ask—is this what you would indicate?—are then the free men of your land really so pure and loving and noble and generous and sincere?"[40] Somewhat cruelly, Whitman did not answer Symonds's letter, but that did not stop Symonds from inquiring again and again over the next two decades about the "Calamus" poems, wondering if he and Whitman were talking about the same thing, namely, what Symonds and others would later refer to as "sexual inversion"—that is, homosexuality.

Finally, in 1890, Whitman did respond. He was brutal. "About the questions on 'Calamus,' *etc.*," Whitman wrote,

> they quite daze me. *Leaves of Grass* is only to be rightly construed by and within its own atmosphere and essential character—all its pages and pieces so coming strictly under. That the "Calamus" part has ever allowed the possibility of such construction as mentioned is terrible. I am fain to hope that the pages themselves are not to be even mentioned for such gratuitous and quite at the time undreamed and unwished

possibility of morbid inferences—which are disavowed by me
and seem damnable.[41]

To further buttress his heterosexual credentials, Whitman
claimed to have fathered six illegitimate children. The children,
of course, did not exist, but even if they did, Whitman seems
not to have known that children alone would not save him or his
poems from the charge of sexual inversion. Symonds, as critics
like to point out, had four children himself.

To many, the letter to Symonds protests entirely too much,
especially the part about the six children, and indeed Whitman
offered a different response to Horace Traubel, who visited the
poet almost daily in the last years of his life and recorded their
conversations. In 1888, before Whitman responded in writing to
Symonds, he discussed the matter with Traubel:

> I often say to myself about Calamus—perhaps it means more
> or less than what I thought myself—means different: perhaps
> I don't know what it all means—perhaps never did know. My
> first instinct about all that Symonds writes is violently reac-
> tionary—is strong and brutal for no, no, no. Then the thought
> intervenes that I maybe do not know all my own meanings: I
> say to myself: "You, too, go away, come back, study your own
> book—an alien or stranger, study your own book, see what it
> amounts to." Sometime or other I will have to write him defini-
> tively about Calamus—give him my word for it what I meant or
> mean it to mean.[42]

Some critics have doubted the sincerity of these com-
ments, too.[43] They believe Whitman knows full well the mean-
ing of "Calamus," but that he pretends otherwise for posterity's
sake. (The same charge, of course, is leveled against his letter

to Symonds.) To my ears, though, it sounds quintessentially Whitman and very plausibly true.

Prior to Symonds's first letter to him and for some time afterward, Whitman conceived of the "Calamus" poems in the language of manly love and adhesiveness. This is what he means when he writes to Symonds that *Leaves of Grass* is "only to be rightly construed by and within its own atmosphere." Its own atmosphere was romantic friendship and phrenology. Beginning in the late 1880s, however, beginning with the invention of homosexuality as a diagnosable pathology, the "Calamus" poems suddenly breathed in a new atmosphere. As a result, they read very differently to Symonds (and, for that matter, to us) than they would have to Whitman and his contemporaries. Whitman, to Traubel at least, admitted the possibility that the old poems may have partaken something of the new atmosphere—that is, they may have truly or also been about homosexuality. At least, he did not rule it out. Even so, I believe Whitman when he insists that what he meant or means is not what Symonds means.

As evidence, consider that even in his most private, most revealing moments, Whitman spoke in the atmospheric language of his day, phrenology. In 1865, Whitman met Peter Doyle, a former Confederate soldier, in Washington, D.C., and the two quickly became very close friends. Their letters survive, and nothing suggests that Whitman and Doyle had sex, but they obviously had a meaningful, at times tumultuous relationship. In a 15 July 1870 entry in his journal, Whitman resolved:

TO GIVE UP ABSOLUTELY *& for good, from the present hour,* *this* FEVERISH, FLUCTUATING, *useless*, UNDIGNIFIED PURSUIT *of 16.4* [Peter Doyle]—*too long, (much too long)* persevered in,—so humiliating— —*It must come at last & had better come now—(It cannot possibly be a success)* LET THERE

FROM THIS HOUR BE NO FALTERING, NO GETTING
at all henceforth, (NOT ONCE, *under any circumstances*)—
avoid seeing her [originally "him"], *or meeting her; or any talk
or explanations—or* ANY MEETING WHATEVER, FROM
THIS HOUR FORTH, FOR LIFE.

. . . .

Depress the adhesive nature/
It is in excess—making life a torment/
Ah this diseased, feverish, disproportionate adhesiveness/[44]

On the one hand, little in the entry suggests anything illicit
or connubial. Whitman speaks only of his "UNDIGNIFIED
PURSUIT," which, strange as it may seem, is still very much the
language of romantic friendship. (Emerson had written some-
thing similar about his Harvard dalliance.) On the other hand,
the codes (16.4 refers to the 16th and 4th letters of the alpha-
bet—that is, PD for Peter Doyle) suggest that Whitman felt he
had something to hide. His changes to the pronouns may reveal
even more. Evidently, he felt his feelings toward Doyle resem-
bled—could even be passed off as—feelings toward a woman. In
his mind, anyway, the line between disproportionate adhesive-
ness and amativeness fades away.

For us, what Whitman calls disproportionate adhesiveness
looks like homosexuality plain and simple. It may not be—again,
we have no evidence that Doyle and Whitman consummated
their relationship or even wanted to—but something neverthe-
less seems to exceed the boundaries of even ardent same-sex
friendship. If we want to conclude from this and other evidence
that Whitman was gay, probably we can.

Keep in mind, though, that the problem is that whatever
Whitman means by "disproportionate adhesiveness," he is dis-
avowing it. As one Whitman scholar has sensibly written, the

language of Whitman's journal entry "indicates that Whitman felt his attraction was excessive, and if this attraction contained any conscious sexual dimensions, these appear to be clearly disapproved of as pathological. In short, what limited extra-textual references we have to Whitman's views on homosexuality . . . are expressions of strong disapproval."[45] In other words, if Whitman was gay, he tried very hard not to be.

As such, his anxiety about his undignified pursuit of Doyle may offer the most insight into Whitman's sexuality. Both in the diary entry and the "Calamus" poems, the language of shame and recrimination seems excessive for something as ordinary and accepted as romantic friendship or everyday adhesiveness. Repeatedly, Whitman apologizes for what he is or does, which does not make sense in a culture that was not especially bothered by manly love. But such confessions make more sense if we grant that Whitman was deeply puzzled about his disproportionate feelings for men. Perhaps adhesiveness and comradeship gave him a way to make sense out of desires that may have otherwise seemed abnormal. As one of his biographers has written, "Whitman had long tried . . . to make his homosexual urges conform as much as possible to permissible same-sex behavior in nineteenth-century America," which sounds right, though I doubt anyone can say whether Whitman's urge toward conformity was as conscious or as calculated as the quotation implies.[46]

Far better, perhaps, is the Freudian language of sublimation, because sublimation is largely a matter of the unconscious. "The sexual life of each one of us," Freud writes in *Fragment of an Analysis of a Case of Hysteria*, "extends to a slight degree—now in this direction, now in that—beyond the narrow lines imposed as the standard of normality."[47] These "perversions," Freud writes, without the judgment such a word implies, are either "suppressed" or, more productively, "diverted to higher, asexual aims" and are therefore "destined to provide the energy for a great number of our cultural achievements."[48] As Freud outlines it, sublimation describes Whitman rather well. He may have suspected that his love for other men exceeded the standard of normality, but he did not suspect it enough to disavow it entirely. Instead, he diverted it—or, to speak the language of the unconscious, it was diverted—into a major cultural achievement, the "Calamus" poems.

That said, we err if we view "Calamus" specifically and comradeship generally as sublimation pure and simple. By that light, the poems and the concept mean little beyond what they reveal—or do not—about Whitman's sexuality. Approaching the poems as hidden expressions of Whitman's homosexuality, we would have to read like psychoanalysts, doing our best to un- or de-sublimate the poems. But that way of reading ignores—or chucks out as mere sublimation—the "political significance" of the "Calamus" poems, which Whitman held to be their "special meaning." Or rather, it chucks out any political significance beyond the homophobia that led Whitman to sublimate his disproportionate adhesiveness in the first place.

In other words, the problem with reading Whitman as a repressed and sublimating gay poet—or "Calamus" as a sequence of repressed and sublimated gay poems—is that they become, merely, gay. We translate Whitman into terms we understand. But I am not convinced that is the best way to read Whitman. In doing so, we make him like us, and that quite frankly is the problem, not the solution.

Instead, perhaps we owe it to Whitman not to try to discover who he really was or who he would have been if he had been us, but rather what he made out of who he thought he was. In other words, perhaps we should not pity Whitman for succumbing to homophobia or for lacking a ready-made way to think about what he called his "adhesiveness," proportionate or disproportionate. Perhaps we should pay even closer attention to what he did say, precisely *because* he lived before we invented a language to talk about these things and, in the process, closed down other ways we might have thought about these and other things.

To put it another way, what kind of nation would we build if, as Whitman urged us to, we took seriously his sense of loving comradeship? What if we did not see it as merely sublimated homosexuality but as a model for gay and straight alike, as Whitman almost certainly intended it to be? What would "the institution of the dear love of comrades" look like? In his service to sick and wounded soldiers during the Civil War, Whitman shows us, and I think we would do well to pay attention and not assume we know better than Whitman what he really meant.

So was Whitman gay? What should I have said to that young woman who asked? If I had it to do over, I would probably say something like this. If by gay, we mean sexual desire for others of the same sex (my dictionary's definition of homosexuality), then yes, a lot of circumstantial evidence suggests that Whitman was gay. But it also matters that Whitman appears never to have thought of himself as gay. At times, he seems to have tried very hard not to be gay.

I would then quickly add the following: instead of asking if Whitman was gay, the better question may be was Whitman queer? And if by queer we mean differing from what is usual or ordinary, especially but not only when it comes to sexuality, then the answer to that question is an unequivocal yes. In fact, we may consider Whitman's queerness his and our blessing. As we shall see in the next chapter, it laid the groundwork for his heroism during the Civil War and his thinking about democracy, and it might yet change how we think about sexual and political life in the United States altogether.

CHAPTER 4

Affection Shall Solve the Problems of Freedom

Those who love each other shall become invincible.
—WALT WHITMAN, "Over the Carnage Rose
a Voice Prophetic" (1867)

In an 1863 letter to his brother Jeff, Walt Whitman called the
Battle at Fredericksburg the "most complete piece of mis-
management perhaps ever yet known in the earth's wars."[1]
At times, Whitman could be rather easily excited, so you have to
take his claim about military history with a grain of salt. Still, if
you wander the battlefield at Fredericksburg, Virginia, as I did
one sunny, chilly day in February, you can almost see what he
means. Even if, like me, you know less than nothing about mili-
tary strategy, from the vantage of the sunken road at the top of
Marye's Heights, overlooking the battlefield below, the Union
campaign at Fredericksburg does indeed begin to look like one
unprecedentedly bad idea after another.

In November 1862, the recently appointed General of
the Army of the Potomac, Ambrose E. Burnside, moved his
troops west toward the undefended city of Fredericksburg.
Burnside hoped to reach Fredericksburg before the scattered
Confederate Army could get there, at which point he could turn
south and march on a direct road to Richmond, Virginia, the

Confederate capital, and thus with any luck bring the war to a swift conclusion.

If not for bad luck, however, Burnside would have had no luck at all. He lost time and men trying to cross the Rappahannock River, which marked the far eastern side of Fredericksburg. And by the time he did cross the river, he faced a Confederate Army that had taken up a nearly impregnable position on the hills behind Fredericksburg. On December 13, Burnside mounted an attack on Lee's right flank, which was fought to a deadly draw. But the real bloodshed came when he tried to attack Lee's forces at Marye's Heights, just beyond the town itself.[2]

In order to reach Lee's heavily dug-in troops and artillery, Union soldiers had to cross four hundred yards of open field. Even today, when three of those four hundred yards are covered by a neighborhood of middle-class houses built around the turn of the twentieth century, you can see just how bad of an idea this was. From noon until dark, Burnside sent wave after wave of Union soldiers toward the Heights, but none got within forty yards of the Confederate line. The field of attack was raked "as with a fine-toothed comb," a Confederate artilleryman reported.[3] A Union soldier recalled: "Our men were slaughtered like sheep. The whole plain was covered with blankets, haversacks, wounded men and dead men."[4] In the course of a single hour of battle, the Union army lost almost 3,000 soldiers. All told, it lost between 6,000 and 8,000 men on that field of the battle. A Virginia infantryman pitied the Union soldiers. "What chance had flesh and blood to carry by storm such a position," he asked, "garrisoned as it was with veteran soldiers? Not one chance in a million."[5] A Confederate artilleryman bragged, "A chicken could not live on that field when we open on it."[6]

But some Union soldiers did beat the odds to survive that day, including George Washington Whitman, younger brother of Walt

The Battle of Fredericksburg looking down from Marye's Heights

Whitman. George Whitman enlisted in the Brooklyn Thirteenth Regiment (later the Fifty-first Regiment) in April of 1861, less than a week after the South fired on Fort Sumter. In the Battle of Fredericksburg, he made the charge against Marye's Heights and, improbably, came away with just a small hole in his cheek. The New York newspapers, however, reported only that George Whitman was among the wounded, not the severity of the wound, or even whether he lived or died. Upon reading this news, and fearing the worst, Walt Whitman set out to find his brother.

Whitman traveled to Fredericksburg by way of Philadelphia, where he had his pocket picked, and then Washington, D.C., where, after endless searching among military hospitals in the city, he received permission to travel to the front in Falmouth, Virginia, just outside Fredericksburg. There, Whitman found his brother, in good health and recently promoted to captain. But Whitman could not ignore the other sights of the camp, which would change utterly the course of his life.

If you got shot during the Civil War, as thousands did during the Battle of Fredericksburg, the bullet did not enter your body and pass cleanly through. Rather, it lodged there, shattering whatever bone it happened to grind its way into. By way of treatment, doctors simply amputated the injured hand, arm, foot, or leg, usually within twenty-four hours of the injury, before the wound could become infected. Outside the field hospitals where doctors performed these surgeries, the amputated limbs tended to pile up. Such was Whitman's first exposure to war. "One of the first things that met my eyes in camp," Whitman wrote his mother in December 1862, "was a heap of feet, arms, legs, & c. under a tree in front of a hospital, the Lacy house."[7]

Used as a field hospital after the Battle of Fredericksburg, the Lacy House, also called Chatham Mansion, still stands, as does the tree that sheltered the heap of amputated limbs. (On my visit, I stood beneath the tree, then felt like an idiot because all I could do was stand there.) After finding his brother, Whitman returned to Lacy House to visit the wounded. In an article published in the *New York Times* in 1864, he recalled the scene in more detail:

Spent a good part of the day in a large brick mansion, on the banks of the Rappahannock, immediately opposite Fredericksburgh. It is used as a hospital since the battle, and seems to have received only the worst cases. Out doors, at the foot of a tree, within ten yards of the front of the house, I notice a heap of amputated feet, legs, arms, hands, &c., about a load for a one-horse cart. Several dead bodies lie near, each covered with its brown woolen blanket. In the door-yard, toward the river, are fresh graves mostly of officers, their names on pieces of barrel-staves or broken board, stuck in the dirt.

The house is quite crowded, everything impromptu, no system, all bad enough, but I have no doubt the best that can be

The Lacy House

done; all the wounds pretty bad, some frightful, the men in their old clothes, unclean and bloody. . . .

I went through the rooms, down stairs and up. Some of the men were dying. I had nothing to give at that visit, but wrote a few letters to folks home, mothers, &c. Also talked to three or four, who seemed most susceptible to it, and needing it.[8]

While the heap of amputated limbs may attract our attention, the more important detail, as far as Whitman's life is concerned, is the men who lay wounded or dying in the hospital. Whitman, it turns out, could not turn his back to such need. He devoted the next three years of his life to meeting it.

Instead of returning to Brooklyn, Whitman lingered for eight or nine days at the front in Virginia and then made his way back to Washington. There he found a job as a copyist in the Office of the Paymaster. By day, he copied government documents. By afternoon and night, he visited sick and wounded soldiers in the dozens of army hospitals that sprouted up in the city. Over the course of the war, Whitman estimated that he visited eighty thousand to a hundred thousand soldiers.

Whitman's devotion to these soldiers matters for a couple of reasons. It inspired some of his most moving poems. It was a heroic act of altruism. But also, and perhaps most important, Whitman's service to sick and wounded soldiers salvaged his hope for democracy in the United States. To understate it considerably, we could use some of that hope today.

Speaking for myself, nothing—not death, not money, not sex—provides such daily doses of malaise as the dysfunctional workings of our democracy and its failure to address—and occasionally even to acknowledge—the most pressing issues of our time. As I began writing the first draft of this chapter, in the wake of the school shooting in Newtown, Connecticut, Congress had just failed to pass even token gun control measures, like expanded background checks for gun buyers, a ban on assault weapons, or a ban on high-capacity magazines. This despite the fact that, as polls showed, an overwhelming majority of Americans support such measures.[9] Not long after, in one of the more bizarre (and smelly) chapters in the history of American democracy, Republicans shut down the government for sixteen days in a last-ditch effort to undo the Patient Protection and Affordable Care Act. Nothing except a great big expensive mess came of it. If, as the great American philosopher John Dewey believed, democracy is a machine for solving the problems a community faces, then as the examples of gun control and the government shutdown suggest, and countless more examples could confirm, our machine is kaput.[10] It lies smoking on the side of the road. You pass it on your way to work.

As it happens, Whitman also suffered serious misgivings about democracy. Although we remember him as the poet of democracy and America, he was also, at times, their harshest critic. In this chapter I explore what saddened and angered Whitman about democracy in his day in order to see whether it bears any resemblance to what saddens and angers us about ours today. Ironically, Whitman found the cure for his malaise about democracy in the Civil War, when actually existing democracy violently and spectacularly failed. Specifically, he found his cure in the army hospitals, where the casualties from democracy's failure washed up. Yet when Whitman describes his hopes for democracy in the United States, he is really just describing what he had already seen in the wards and among the wounded soldiers of the army hospitals. I ask what Whitman saw in those great army hospitals that sustained his faith in democracy. I do so in the hopes that it might sustain ours, too.

In later years, Whitman liked to say that the war saved him.[11] When it comes to our ailing faith in democracy in the United States, Whitman in the war could well save us.

I.

Man is a political animal, Aristotle wrote, and Whitman, strange as it may seem, was no exception.[12] In his twenties, he was making a nice career for himself in the Democratic Party machine that ruled New York City. He published his early poems and short stories in their newspapers. He stumped for their presidential candidates. He once addressed a crowd of fifteen thousand at a party rally in City Hall Park. He wrote for and edited their newspapers, including the *Brooklyn Daily Eagle*. He even knew his way around Tammany Hall.

But slavery drove a wedge between Whitman and his party. Whitman belonged to the "Barnburner" faction of the Democrats, which opposed the extension of slavery into the western territories the United States acquired during the Mexican War. By contrast, the "Hunker" faction sided with Southern Democrats who hoped to expand slavery beyond the South. When the Hunkers won control of the Democratic Party, Whitman was politically vulnerable. In 1848, he was fired from his post as editor of the *Daily Eagle*. As a result, Whitman lost his taste for the compromises and betrayals of organized politics. From 1849 to 1855, except for one or two poems aimed at Doughfaces, Northern Democrats who favored the interests of Southern slaveholders, for the most part Whitman retired from politicking and journalism.

Of course, the poetry Whitman composed during the first half of 1850s had a political shade, including his unequivocal denunciations of slavery, his seemingly infinite capacity to sympathize with others, and his cheerleading for liberty, equality, and democracy. On the eve of the Civil War, too, he brought out the third edition of *Leaves of Grass*, which he hoped would hold the country together when all else—courts, constitutions, force—failed.

Despite going silent on most matters political for most of the 1850s, Whitman did eventually return to the subject in a remarkable series of essays written in the second half of the 1860s, which he later brought out as a book in 1871 called *Democratic Vistas*. In that book, he has some astonishingly jaundiced things to say about the state of democracy in his time. Before turning to what Whitman thought would save American democracy from its illnesses, then, it is worth exploring what he thought was making it sick—and might even finish it off.

Writing in the aftermath of the Civil War, Whitman worried that the United States would remain internally divided, something less than a fully integrated nation. "The fear of conflicting and irreconcilable interiors, and the lack of a common skeleton, knitting all close," Whitman writes, "continually haunts me."[13] No "fervid and tremendous IDEA," as Whitman put it, held the country together.[14] And the one idea that did seem to hold the country together, its devotion to material prosperity, struck him as shortsighted, a means without an end.

In addition to the irreconcilable conflict between regions of the country, Whitman also feared the irreconcilable conflict that he saw developing between groups *within* the same regions of the country. Prophetically, Whitman could see the clashes between workers and employers that would soon, in less than a decade, overwhelm the country. (In 1877, a local railroad strike developed into the first national strike in American history. By the end of it, a hundred people had died and millions of dollars in property had been destroyed. Things only got worse after that.) "Even to-day," Whitman writes, "amid these whirls . . . that problem, the labor question, begin[s] to open like a yawning gulf, rapidly widening every year."[15] "What prospect have we?" he asks, already sounding defeated.[16] In the original edition of the book, he was even grimmer. "The immense problem of the relation, adjustment, conflict, between Labor and its status and pay, on the one side, and the Capital of employers on the other side—loom[s] up over These States like an ominous, limitless, murky cloud, perhaps before long to overshadow all."[17]

In addition to the Labor Question, Whitman worried about what he elsewhere referred to as the Poverty Question. By the Poverty Question, he meant the crucial but unanswered question of whether democracy could coexist with large numbers of what he calls "the very poor, the ignorant, and . . . those out of business."[18] He somewhat improbably lumps these figures together because, for him, they have no attachment to the country, no concern for it, and vice versa. As I discussed in the second chapter,

Whitman believed that democracy required prosperous citizens because only those who have an economic stake in a country will have a political stake in it. His analogy, as usual, was the celestial forces of the universe. Planets in a far-flung solar system are held together by gravity. In a far-flung democracy like the United States, something—for Whitman, shared prosperity—would need to hold otherwise diffuse individuals together. If it did not, if people were left out of prosperity—if, that is, they were poor— then they would float free of the gravitational hold of others and their nation. The poor would have, or so Whitman feared, no attraction toward their country, and the country, in turn, no attraction toward them. Through no fault of their own, the poor made for poor citizens, and their indifference to politics impoverished democracy.

Whitman has one more serious concern, which I address in a moment, but I should pause here to note that his misgivings will, alas, ring loudly true today. We too have been haunted by the ghost of conflicting and irreconcilable interiors. For proof, look no further than our maps of blue and red states, memorably rendered after the 2004 Presidential Election as "The United States of Canada" and "Jesusland." To be sure, those maps exaggerate our regional differences. Not everyone in Pickens County, Georgia, votes for a Republican president, and not everyone in Berkshire Country, Massachusetts, votes for a Democratic one. And most people, in most states, say that religion is important to their lives. More accurate maps show pockets of blue and pockets of red amid a sea of deep, dark purple. Still, many of us cannot quite shake the sense that the West Coast, the upper Midwest, and the Northeast constitute one country, and that the interior, including the South, constitutes another. At times, especially when the solid South reports its election results, it can feel like the Civil War never ended. Rather, to reverse the famous von Clausewitz maxim, politics simply became the continuation of war by other means.

Those regions perhaps feel divided because the political parties that by and large represent them *have* definitively grown more divided. At no point in recent history have Democrats thought less of Republicans and Republicans thought less of Democrats. As Whitman feared, no fervid and tremendous IDEA holds us together—unless you count our self-righteous contempt for one another.

True, most of us, Democrats and Republicans, Northerners and Southerners, come together in a heartfelt if vaguely articulated devotion to liberal democracy, and we should not underestimate that shared commitment. But like a commitment to material prosperity, a commitment to liberal democracy can seem like a means without a clearly articulated end. No doubt some may prefer it that way. The great advantage of liberal democracy is that it leaves each of us more or less free to pursue the ends we feel deserve our efforts. But liberal democracy can also leave us, as Whitman feared, without a common skeleton, with nothing, no virtue or set of virtues, to knit us together. We lack, as Whitman put it, a "moral identity."[19] Americans may revere one moral foundation or another—selflessness, fairness, loyalty, respect for authority, respect for the sacred—but we cannot agree on a single one or a single cocktail of them all.[20] To that extent, we remain a democracy, but not a country that represents anything more than the combined and competing self-interests of its inhabitants.

To be sure, we have made some progress in the other realms of which Whitman despaired. As Whitman imagined it, the labor question no longer overshadows all. Workers strike less often than they ever have, and when they do, they do not, as they did starting in 1877, get shot by the hundreds or destroy property by the millions. Yet that does not mean the labor question is a settled one. It has simply settled down. Instead, we have class inequalities without the class conflict. We still struggle with the question of workers and their status and pay—and what this question means for democracy. As legions of journalists, economists, and protesters almost constantly remind us, economic inequality in the United States has risen to levels not seen for almost a century.

Much the same could be said for the Poverty Question. Here, what Whitman feared has largely come to pass. As measured by voting, the poor remain only marginally connected to their country. Among eligible voters aged 25 to 44 who live in families with incomes below $20,000, only 43 percent reported having voted in November of 2012. By contrast, nearly 80 percent of eligible voters aged 25 to 44 who live in families with incomes above $150,000 said they voted.[21] For Whitman, this disparity matters. A majority of the very poor do not participate in the selection of those who will represent them in government. It should not surprise us then that their interests, for the most part, go unrepresented. But it should concern us, as it did Whitman, that a majority of the poor would feel so little connection to their democracy that they could not be bothered to vote. By Whitman's standard, any such democracy is a failure, one in name only.

III.

To most of us, much of this—the divided American public, the economic and political inequalities of modern American democracy—will not come as a great surprise. Moreover, most of us will readily agree with Whitman that such things are blots on our democracy. Below, I let Whitman have his say about how he thinks we ought to clear up such blots, though like most critics he is better at spotting problems than solving them. By far, though, the most surprising part of Whitman's diagnosis of democracy in his day—and one that still surprises today—is not what he has to say about the divisions in American democracy, whether between regions or between classes, but what he has to say about the American people in and of themselves.

Whitman has a well-deserved reputation as the champion of the common man. But by the second half of the1860s, when he wrote *Democratic Vistas*, he had his doubts—to say the least— about the people, about the ordinary Americans who would form American democracy. Whitman tells us that he wrote *Democratic Vistas* after reading the Scottish philosopher Thomas Carlyle's 1867 essay, "Shooting Niagara: And After?" In the essay, Carlyle attacks what he calls "swarmery." By swarmery, Carlyle means what we would today call groupthink. For Carlyle, the Swarm, the conventional wisdom, more than anything else championed Democracy. But they had no real basis for that belief, Carlyle charges, only faith that it must be so. Writing in response to the Reform Act of 1867, which extended the vote in England to most workers in towns and cities, Carlyle attacked both democracy and those who reflexively swore by it:

> Inexpressibly delirious seems to me, at present in my solitude, the puddle of Parliament and Public upon what it calls the "Reform Measure;" that is to say, the calling in of new supplies of blockheadism, gullibility, bribeability, amenability to beer and balderdash, by way of amending the woes we have had from our previous supplies of that bad article.[22]

When you define democracy as "blockheadism, gullibility, bribeability, and amenability to beer and balderdash," you will not likely think—as Carlyle did not—that the more the better. To put it another way, Carlyle asserts that the cure for what ails

England—"the universal rottenness, and quagmire of mendaci-
ties"—is surely not what sickened it in the first place.[23] You do
not treat cancer with more cancer, and for Carlyle, democracy is
just that, a cancer. It is a malignant growth that starts small but
soon spreads to the rest of the body politic, destroying life as it
progresses. Under democracy, Carlyle fears, "every question and
interest of mankind" was to be decided by "Count of Heads," but
nothing guaranteed that might (a majority) would equal right.[24]
Just the opposite. Foolishness, Carlyle believed, not wisdom,
usually resided in the crowd.

Think what you will about Carlyle, he is right about one
thing: no one says this about democracy anymore. At least not
out loud. No one did then, either. And whereas Whitman ulti-
mately disagrees with Carlyle over the wisdom—or lack thereof—
of democracy, he concedes that he shares some of Carlyle's mis-
givings. "I was at first roused to much anger and abuse by this
essay from Mr. Carlyle," Whitman writes, "so insulting to the
theory of America—but happening to think afterwards how I had
more than once been in the like mood, during which his essay
was evidently cast, and seen persons and things in the same light,
(indeed some might say there are signs of the same feeling in
these Vistas)—I have since read it again . . . with respect."[25]

If anything, Whitman understates how much his mood in
Democratic Vistas at times resembles Carlyle's. Indeed, his denun-
ciations of democracy and its various constituents come as a shock.
Early on, sounding very much like Carlyle, he acknowledges "the
people's crudeness, vice, caprices."[26] Later, in a long passage that
occurs early in the book, he expands on these criticisms:

> Society, in these States, is canker'd, crude, superstitious, and
> rotten. Political, or law-made society, is also. In any vigor,
> the element of the moral conscience, the most important, the

verteber to State or man, seems to me either entirely lacking, or seriously enfeebled or ungrown.[27]

Yet Whitman was just warming to his theme. He continues:

I say we had best look our times and lands searchingly in the face, like a physician diagnosing some deep disease. Never was there, perhaps, more hollowness at heart than at present, and here in the United States. Genuine belief seems to have left us. The underlying principles of the States not believ'd in, (for all this hectic glow, and these melo-dramatic screamings), nor is humanity itself believ'd in. What penetrating eye does not everywhere see through the mask? The spectacle is appalling.[28]

Whitman tells us that he has it on good authority, from "an acute and candid person, in the revenue department in Washington, who is led by the course of his employment to regularly visit the cities, north, south, and west, to investigate frauds," that

the depravity of the business classes of our country is not less than has been supposed, but infinitely greater. The official services of America, national, state, and municipal, in all their branches and departments, except the judiciary, are saturated in corruption, bribery, falsehood, mal-administration.

And just when you find yourself grateful that at least the judiciary escapes Whitman's wrath, he adds: "and the judiciary is tainted."[29] Shoot. "The great cities," Whitman writes, "reek with respectable as much as non-respectable robbery and scoundrelism."[30] "The best class we show," he says, after attacking those interested in nothing but "pecuniary gain," "is but a mob of fashionably dress'd speculators and vulgarians."[31]

But it gets worse. Everyone expects government and business-men to disappoint. No surprises there. No, what truly shocks a reader of Whitman's essay is what he says about the common man. "Confess," he writes, as though willing himself and his readers to admit something they would rather not,

> that to severe eyes, using the moral microscope upon humanity, a sort of dry and flat Sahara appears, these cities, crowded with petty grotesques, malformations, phantoms, playing meaning-less antics. Confess that everywhere, in shop, street, church, theatre, bar-room, official chair, are pervading flippancy and vulgarity, low cunning, infidelity—everywhere the youth puny, impudent, foppish, prematurely ripe—everywhere an abnormal libidousness, unhealthy forms, male, female, painted, padded, dyed, chignon'd, muddy complexions, bad blood, the capacity for good motherhood deceasing or deceas'd, shallow notions of beauty, with a range of manners, or rather lack of manners, (considering the advantages enjoy'd), probably the meanest to be seen in the world.[32]

In truth, I find it hard to believe that Whitman could write these passages, especially the last. It seems so out of character; so petty, so prim, and so full of contempt. Abnormal libidousness? This from a man who boasted of making love to his own soul?[33] And lack of manners? From a man who claimed to "cock my hat as I please indoors or out"?[34] Where is the poet who speaks lov-ingly of the "divine average"?[35] Where is the Whitman who heard America singing? Gone, apparently, washed away by the stench given off by American democracy and the infidels and jezebels who constitute it.

Perhaps I do not want to believe that Whitman wrote these passages because these doubts about the people hit a little too close to home. From day to day, I might lament what the filibuster and gerrymandering are doing to democracy in the United States, or marvel at how far off the rails the Republican Party can apparently go. And I might further bemoan how, as a result of all these developments, little gets done in our democracy concerning the problems that we do talk about, like unemployment and the deficit, and even less gets done about the truly perilous problems besetting our country, like childhood poverty, economic inequality, and global warming, to name but three of the injustices and ticking time bombs we currently face. Yet every so often, usually come election season, or when I think about the audience for reality TV or, worse, the hordes eager to take their turn on it, or if I wander into a Walmart, I stumble onto a less comforting thought. Namely, that perhaps the common man (and woman) is not as noble or as wise as I have wanted to think or been led to believe.

This elitism mortifies me, not least because it cuts against the grain of everything I hold dear. Many of us on the political left, and I am guiltier than most, might as well be stuck in the 1930s, when every man is a Forgotten Man and no populism can possibly be populist enough. My heart flutters every time I see Norman Rockwell's *Freedom of Speech* painting from 1943, with its undistinguished yet Lincoln-esque common man rising to address, humbly but no doubt wisely, his fellow citizens at a town hall meeting, and I would rather not think about how the portrait may distort reality. (Today, that man is likely to bring an assault weapon to the meeting.) In other words, for those of us raised on Howard Zinn's *A People's History of the United States*, in which angelic common men and women battle diabolic capitalists and their racist minions, it pains us to be reminded, especially from someone like Whitman, that the world does not divide as neatly as we would like between the noble and the barbaric, the pure and the rotten, the good and the bad, the folk and the elite. People can inspire you, but they can also disappoint you.

IV.

At first glance *Democratic Vistas* does not save your vision of democracy—it sours it still further. Whitman describes exactly how democracy fails, and you realize that it has continued to fail in much the same ways since he wrote about it over 150 years ago. Rather than relieving our malaise about democracy in the United States, Whitman piles it on. If American democracy disgusted someone as sanguine as Whitman, what chance do I have?

Yet Whitman did not write *Democratic Vistas* just to air his grievances against democracy, or to stoke our occasional dismay at the benighted antics of everyday God-fearing Americans. Rather, dismay is simply his starting place. In general, Whitman seeks to defend democracy from critics like Carlyle and from the cynical and misanthropic moods that Whitman occasionally shares with Carlyle. Happily, in doing so, he does ease us of some of our worst fears about democracy.

Given all that Whitman observes about the failings of democracy in the United States, and the failings of its ordinary citizens, you might wonder how he can possibly go on to defend American democracy. Yet defend democracy he does, and the answer as to how, given the aspersions he casts on the present, and the people who make it up, lies in his title: *Democratic Vistas*, with an emphasis on *Vista*, the long view, the far-off.

Ingeniously, Whitman argues that the justification for democracy is not that people can wisely rule themselves now, today, but that democracy will give people the opportunity to develop into

Norman Rockwell, Freedom of Speech, *1943*

the kind of people who *can* wisely rule themselves tomorrow, or someday anyway. "We endow the masses with the suffrage," he writes, "for their own sake."[36] Refuse them that opportunity, though, and they will remain as "full of perverse maleficence" as ever, and as unfit to rule as ever.[37] That is, Whitman does not so much defend actually existing democracy in the United States as he defends what democracy might develop into in the future.[38] "America," he writes at the outset of the book, "counts, as I reckon, for her justification and success (for who, as yet, dare claim success?) almost entirely on the future," adding, "Nor, is that hope unwarranted."[39]

Whitman can look to the future because he thinks the present has gotten some things right. Like many other people, then and now, Whitman thinks that when it comes to the form of government you could not do much better than representative democracy. Whitman believes that the United States is not likely to improve on what he calls "the political foundation rights of immense masses of people."[40] He reveres "the Declaration of Independence and, as it began and has now grown, with its amendments, the Federal Constitution."[41]

Unlike those who might agree with him on this point, Whitman does not believe that representative democracy triumphs over other forms of government because it maintains order, secures property, or enables material prosperity, nor even because it honors the inalienable rights of man. It does do these things, but, to be judged a success, it has to do more. It has to create a thoroughly democratic culture, the purpose of which, in turn, would be to create thoroughly democratic citizens. "The President is up there in the White House for you," Whitman writes in an early poem, "it is not you who are here for him," and he means, of course, that the government, including the President, is supposed to represent you, not the other way around.[42] As Lincoln put it in the Gettysburg Address, in lines that Whitman immediately recognized as brilliant, we have "government of the people, by the people, and for the people." But Whitman placed special emphasis on the "for the people" part of that equation. Government exists, he believes, and the President is up there in the White House, for your sake, to enable your development. Only democracy can give individuals the opportunity—and the responsibility—to develop as individuals.

This is why Whitman is so concerned, in *Democratic Vistas* and elsewhere, with the moral conscience (or its lack thereof) among ordinary Americans—because that is the final proof of democracy. He believes that "mentality, taste, belief" matter "far more than the popular political suffrage" and produce "results inside and underneath the elections of Presidents or Congresses."[43] In other words, who we are, and not who or what we vote for, is what truly matters. And who we are matters because if you get the character right, everything else—voting, lawmaking, and law-enforcing— will come out right, too. "That which really balances and conserves the social and political world," he says, "is not so much legislation, police, treaties, and dread of punishment, as the latent eternal intuitional sense, in humanity, of fairness, manliness, decorum, &c."[44] To put it another way, laws do not keep the peace, stop the rush to war, or build a just society. People do.

Below I say which virtues, and which ones in particular, Whitman thought made for a good character, and for a good democracy. For the moment, however, what matters is how Whitman thought those virtues would come about: who made them, where they came from, and how—and who—the people would learn them from.

The answer to the question of where virtues would come from, laughable as it may seem, is poets. And Whitman is dead serious. In fact, if you look hard, you can almost see his point. If, like Whitman, you believe that who people are matters for democracy far more than whom they vote for, and that voting might even be the least part of democracy, then you will take more than a passing interest in how people form their characters. For Whitman, this formation happens in and through the family, which explains what, to our ears, seems like his creepy obsession with motherhood in *Democratic Vistas*. Equally important, he believed people formed their characters in and through culture, which made it more important than perhaps anyone suspected.

Whitman acknowledges the many forms of culture that shape people: art, schools, theology, theater, oratory. But he thinks that literature matters the most: "Few are aware how the great literature penetrates all, gives hue to all, shapes aggregates and individuals, and, after subtle ways, with irresistible power, constructs, sustains, demolishes, at will."[45] To most observers, Whitman writes, world history seems to turn on big events: wars, uprisings, downfalls, new inventions, and the doings of heroic figures. "These of course play their part," he admits, "yet it may be a single new thought, imagination, abstract principle, even literary style, fit for the time, put in shape by some great literatus, and projected among mankind, may duly cause changes, growths, removals, greater than the longest and bloodiest war, or the most stupendous merely political, dynastic, or commercial overturn."[46] In short, ideas matter. And the creator of ideas matters, too.

Poets, Percy Shelley observed in a phrase Whitman would have eagerly endorsed, are the unacknowledged legislators of the world. The problem for Whitman is that though the United States may have evolved politically beyond feudalism, its culture, including its poetry, remained thoroughly feudal. For example, Whitman reveres Shakespeare. But he thinks that Shakespeare, like the other artists and writers of the feudal past, is "poisonous to the idea of the pride and dignity of the common people, the life-blood of democracy."[47] He is "artist and singer of feudalism in its sunset."[48] Shakespeare, however, is just the tip of the iceberg: "The models of our literature, as we get it from other lands, ultramarine, have had their birth in courts, and bask'd and grown in castle sunshine; all smells of prince's favors."[49] By "ultramarine," Whitman simply means coming from beyond the sea, and to him, that is the problem.

"What has fill'd, and fills to-day our intellect, our fancy" he writes, "furnishing the standards therein, is yet foreign."[50] Even his contemporary artists and writers, Whitman observes, remain in thrall to feudalism. "Do you call those genteel little creatures American poets? Do you term that perpetual, pistareen, paste-pot work, American art, American drama, taste, verse?" He responds, answering his own question, "I think I hear, echoed as from some mountaintop afar in the west, the scornful laugh of the Genius of these States."[51]

Therefore, what the country needed, what the age demanded, was not Shakespeare or genteel little American poets but what Whitman calls "the poet of the modern."[52] In short, democratic poets for a democratic people. "Our fundamental want to-day in the United States," he believes,

> with closest, amplest reference to present conditions, and to the future, is of a class, and the clear idea of a class, of native authors, literatures, far different, far higher in grade than any yet known, sacerdotal, modern, fit to cope with our occasions, lands, permeating the whole mass of American mentality, taste, belief, breathing into it a new breath of life, giving it decision . . . radiating, begetting appropriate teachers, schools, manners, and, as its grandest result, accomplishing . . . a religious and moral character beneath the political and productive and intellectual bases of the States.[53]

Whitman's metaphor is of foundations. A nation without a great literature is like a house without a foundation. Neither will stand for long. "For know you not, dear, earnest reader," he continues, "that the people of our land may all read and write, and may all possess the right to vote—and yet the main things may be entirely lacking?"[54] For Whitman, poets would supply the main things.

V.

Alas, Whitman's appeal to the future and to the poets may not
reassure you about American democracy. Speaking as the vista
toward which Whitman looked, democracy in our time does not
differ all that much from democracy in his, and this may darken
the mood considerably. If Whitman perceived these problems
(regional and class divisions, the moral turpitude of the people)
in his day, and they continue to bedevil us, then the outlook has
not improved. To switch metaphors, these must not be bugs in
the democratic software but features. If we endowed the masses
with suffrage for their own sake, as Whitman argued, it is not
altogether clear what uses they have made of it. For anyone who
follows American politics closely, the spectacle is still appalling.

Worse still, not only have we failed to arrive where Whitman
said we must. His hope for what would take us there, poetry,
has not fared well, either. If you think about it for any time at all,
Whitman's argument seems absurd. The spectacle of American
democracy, then and now, is appalling, and the cure for this spec-
tacle is . . . poetry? Why not juggling? Or baking? Or line danc-
ing? At least Americans like those things. And I say that as some-
one who loves poetry and who tries to share that love with others.
But what I have learned from my attempt to share it with others,
at least in the classroom, is that it is hard enough to get people to
read poetry, let alone understand it, let alone let it alter who they
are and, far down the road, whom they vote for.

In sum, if our hopes for a balanced budget, ending poverty,
and surviving global warming rely on poets, God help us.

So Whitman's thesis has some problems. Nevertheless, I think
there is something to what he says. To start, Whitman's theory
of democracy would invite us to shift our attention away from
the back-and-forth of everyday political life and toward the more

fundamental issue of character, and I find that change of outlook extraordinarily refreshing. Like Whitman, we might be better off taking the long view. (At last, that reason you have been looking for not to read the *New York Times*!) After all, if Whitman is right, what truly influences politics in a democracy is character, and character does not change over the course of a day, week, month, or even an election cycle. It changes over the course of a generation, and it changes in unpredictable ways and for unpredictable reasons. In other words, we could, following Whitman, take our eye off the effect (daily political life) and focus on the cause (the character of the American people). The view may be no better, but it could not be much worse.

Further, if Whitman is right that intuition and character ultimately matter, then perhaps he is also right that poets—or culture more generally—are indeed the unacknowledged legislators of the world. How do people form the intuitions that lie behind their beliefs? At least in part from what they read, especially when they are young. Or from their parents, who also draw on what they read. So what and who should they read? Poets, says Whitman, and perhaps we should not laugh so quickly. After all, he is essentially describing the premise of this book in general and this chapter in particular. Our democracy is ailing. What do our poets have to say?

You can try this out for yourself. For example, what kind of person would you be if you read Whitman's poetry? You can guess based on the previous chapters of this book. For Whitman, an ideal democratic citizen—and a careful reader of his poetry— would intuitively believe in the immortality of the soul and not fear death. Why might this matter? Whitman believed that, in addition to getting the metaphysics wrong, conventional religions did not instill independence and self-reliance in their practitioners, virtues that were crucial for democracy. An ideal democratic citizen would value money and making money but also know its limits. He or she would know enough not to devote his or her life to it. And an ideal democratic citizen would believe in the sanctity of our bodies and our sexuality and use them accordingly. Moreover, an ideal citizen would recognize that the communal nature of our bodies—remember "every atom belonging to me as good belongs to you"—means we are more or less equal, at least when it comes to what (our souls, our bodies, our status as citizens) matters the most. We would not believe that anyone was intrinsically better than anyone else or had more or less right to anything on earth than anyone else. An ideal American citizen, that is, would swear by equality.

Would our democracy be better off if each of us believed these things? Would our fights over taxes and gay marriage burn off like the morning fog? Possibly, but you could believe what Whitman tells you and still think that taxes are robbery by another name, that government has grown too big, or that the poor leech off the rest of us.

Yet there is one more virtue that Whitman articulates in his poetry that, if taken seriously, would do more to cure our democracy of its various ills than any other virtue he describes. Whitman referred to this virtue by various names: adhesiveness, companionship, comradeship, manly love. He developed it over the course of the "Calamus" sequence of poems, and he developed it on the eve of and in response to the divisions portended by the Civil War. As late as *Democratic Vistas*, he still described it as essential for democracy: "It is to the development, identification, and general prevalence of that fervid comradeship that I look for the counterbalance and offset of our materialistic and vulgar American democracy, and for the spiritualization thereof."[55] Indeed, when Whitman tries to imagine what America would look like in one hundred years, he predicts that "comradeship" will be "fully express'd." He believes that it, and nothing else, "promised . . . the most substantial hope and safety of the future of these States."[56]

What is more, he believed he had witnessed the flowering of comradeship on the battlefields and especially in the hospitals of the Civil War, where he spent countless hours tending sick and wounded soldiers. To see what he means by comradeship, our hope and safety, let us, like Whitman, go and make our hospital visit.

VI.

Since opening in 1840, the Patent Office Building in downtown Washington, half a dozen blocks east of the White House and just north of the Mall, has done many duties. It began life by housing and displaying models of the thousands of patents the federal government issued over the years. In the 1840s, it was also a "Museum of Curiosities." Tourists came to see the original Declaration of Independence, Benjamin Franklin's printing press, George Washington's sword, and Andrew Jackson's uniform. In the 1850s, the Patent Office Building expanded and took in other offices under the Department of the Interior: the General Land Office, Pension Office, Census Bureau, and Office of Indian Affairs. (For about six months in 1865, until he was fired for being the author of an indecent book, Whitman worked as a copyist for the Office of Indian Affairs. His desk was in the basement of the East Wing of the Patent Office Building.) In March 1865, the building hosted President Lincoln's second inaugural ball. In 1932, the Patent Office left the building, and the Civil Service Commission moved in. In 1955, President Eisenhower saved the building from demolition, and today it is home to the

The U.S. Patent Office, ca. 1855

Smithsonian American Art Museum and the National Portrait Gallery.[57]

Interesting as they are, none of these purposes, not even Whitman's basement office, drew me to the building in the middle of a long, gray Washington winter. Instead, I came because the Patent Office Building is one of the last, and certainly the grandest, of the buildings that served as a military hospital during the Civil War. From late 1861 to April 1863, thousands of sick and wounded soldiers, including casualties from the Battle of Fredericksburg, passed through the building, lying in cots among the cases displaying patent models. It was also in the Patent Office Building—and other, now destroyed hospitals— that Whitman began his service to sick and wounded soldiers during the Civil War.

In one of his first articles for the *New York Times*, in February 1863, Whitman described the scene:

A few weeks ago the vast area of the second story of that noblest of Washington buildings, the Patent office, was crowded close

Soldiers lying in bunks in the Patent Office before the
building was turned into a hospital (1861)

with rows of sick, badly wounded, and dying soldiers. They
were placed in three very large apartments. I went there sev-
eral times. It was a strange, solemn, and, with all its features
of suffering and death, a sort of fascinating sight. I went some-
times at night to soothe and relieve particular cases; some, I
found, needed a little cheering up and friendly consolation at
that time, for they went to sleep better afterwards. Two of the
immense apartments are filled with high and ponderous glass
cases crowded with models in miniature of every kind of uten-
sil, machine, or invention it ever entered into the mind of man
to conceive, and with curiosities and foreign presents. Between
these cases were lateral openings, perhaps eight feet wide, and
quite deep, and in these were placed many of the sick; besides a
great long double row of them up and down through the middle
of the hall. Many of them were very bad cases, wounds and
amputations. Then there was a gallery running above the hall,
in which there were beds also. It was, indeed, a curious scene at
night when lit up. The glass cases, the beds, the sick, the gallery
above and the marble pavement under foot; the suffering, and

the fortitude to bear it in the various degrees; occasionally, from
some, the groan that could not be repressed; sometimes a poor
fellow dying, with emaciated face and glassy eyes, the nurse by
his side, the doctor also there, but no friends, no relative—such
were the sights but lately in the Patent office.[58]

That last detail—that the poor fellow died with "no friends,
no relative"—seems to have touched Whitman the most, for soon
enough he would commit his life to befriending these soldiers.

In his journal from this period, he jotted a couple of notes
from his January visit to the Patent Office Hospital:

> Patent Office Hospital Ward 1 & 2—bed 53 James E.
> Woodmansee (co. C 114th N.Y. Rev. Ray Woodmansee
> Norwich Chenango co. N.Y.
> 61. Camp. (something to read a good book)
> Saml. F Taries co. G 1st Delaware
> + 27 wants some figs and a book and some cakes ginger
> + 23 & 24 wants some horehound candy[59]

The entry was obviously written quickly, but you can tell
a great deal about what Whitman did in the hospitals from it.
The first is an address. Presumably, James Woodmansee asked
Whitman to write his family, who likely did not know that he was
wounded or how he fared. (Norwich is the county seat of Chenago
County, New York.) "Camp." probably means Campbell, who
apparently wanted "something to read a good book," as did the
soldier in bed 27, who also wanted some figs and cakes ginger.
Whitman seems to have merely noted Samuel F. Taries's name,
perhaps so he would remember him on subsequent visits. The
soldiers in beds 23 and 24, meanwhile, wanted some horehound
candy, a throat lozenge. Usually, on his return visit, a day or a few

days later, Whitman would bring the men what they asked for. As these entries suggest, he was less a nurse to the soldiers, and more a wandering friend. It suited him perfectly.

By the end of the war, Whitman estimated that he had made some six hundred visits like the one he made to the Patent Office Hospital in January 1863. On each visit, he performed many of the same tasks. He would hand out paper and stamped envelopes so soldiers could write home, or he would write letters for those who could not. He handed out tobacco, newspapers, fruit, and small sums of money. He lent out books. Once, on a hot day in June, he bought ten gallons of ice cream and distributed it among the patients of Carver Hospital. He paid for the gifts out of his own salary, and others raised money on his behalf, though his reputation sometimes hurt his cause. Ralph Waldo Emerson tried (and failed) to raise money from among his Boston circle for Whitman's hospital work. "There is a prejudice ag[ain]st you here among the 'fine ladies' & gentlemen of the transcendental School," Emerson's friend, James Redpath, wrote Whitman, reporting on Emerson's efforts. "It is believed that you are not ashamed enough of your reproductive organs."[60]

The most important aid Whitman offered, however, usually required no money at all. Occasionally, he would dress wounds. (His moving poem "The Wound Dresser" is about just this.) To those who asked, he would, he reported, offer "passages from the Bible, expounding them, prayer at the bedside, explanations of doctrine, & c." Of this last service, he knowingly observed, "I think I see my friends smiling at this confession, but I was never more in earnest in my life."[61] (The joke is that though Whitman had a spiritual side, he was never a conventional Christian.) He would declaim poems, though never his own. (He seems to have told no one of his own poems.) With a large group of soldiers, he played Twenty Questions.

Often, he simply sat with soldiers who, sick or wounded, far-away from home, some for the first time in their lives, were understandably frightened and dejected. "Most of them," Whitman observed of the soldiers, "are entirely without friends or acquaintances here—no familiar face, and hardly a word of judicious sympathy or cheer, through their sometimes long and tedious sickness, or the aggravated pangs of their wounds."[62] More than anything else, Whitman offered soldiers judicious sympathy and cheer. In short, he gave himself.

His accounts of these scenes are heartrending. In his *Memoranda During the War*, published in 1875 but drawn mostly from his notebooks and diaries of the period, he writes:

> In one bed a young man, Marcus Small, Co. K, Seventh Maine—sick with dysentery and typhoid fever—pretty critical, too—I talk with him often—he thinks he will die—looks like it indeed. I write a letter for him home to East Livermore, Maine—I let him talk to me a little, but not much, advise him to keep very quiet—do most of the talking myself—stay quite awhile with him, as he holds on to my hand—talk to him in a cheering, but slow, low, and measured manner—talk about his furlough, and going home as soon as he is able.[63]

Like most soldiers in the Washington hospitals, Marcus Small fought for the North, but Whitman visited everyone, even those from the South. Although he despised the political leaders of the South, whom he blamed, along with spineless politicians in the North, for causing what he invariably referred to as the Secession War, Whitman could not withhold sympathy from Southern soldiers, who, wounded and captured on the battlefield, also washed up in Washington hospitals. "I staid tonight a long time," Whitman writes,

Mathew Brady's photograph of Walt Whitman, ca. 1862

by the bed-side of a new patient, a young Baltimorean, aged about 19 years, W.S.P., (2nd Md. Southern,) very feeble, right leg amputated, can't sleep hardly at all—has taken a great deal of morphine, which, as usual, is costing more than it comes to. Evidently very intelligent and well bred—very affectionate— held on to my hand, and put it by his face, not willing to let me leave. As I was lingering, soothing him in his pain, he says to me suddenly, "I hardly think you know who I am—I don't wish to impose upon you—I am a rebel soldier." I said I did not know that, but it made no difference........ Visiting him daily for about two weeks after that, while he lived (death had mark'd him, and he was quite alone,) I loved him much, always kiss'd him, and he did me.[64]

Both too much, and not enough, can be made of these ges- tures of affection between Whitman and hospitalized soldiers.

As I detail in the chapter on Whitman's sexuality, such gestures between men, while not exactly common, were not unusual, either. In any case, few people seem to have thought of them as sexual, and that context seems even less appropriate here. To be sure, as I will underscore in a moment, Whitman relished the affection he could show to these young men, and the affection they showed him in return. In one or two cases, he seems to have formed close personal relationships with soldiers he visited in the hospitals and who subsequently recovered from their wounds or illnesses. And it is true enough that his thinking about "adhesiveness," manly love, and comradeship prepared him well to offer the affection that soldiers apparently needed and returned. But I doubt very much, as critics sometimes imply, that Whitman held the hands of dying young men because he viewed it as an opportunity to act on his homosexual impulses, and the suggestion that he did seems to cheapen what he did do, which is to comfort very lonely, very scared young men.[65]

Given the time he spent with them, Whitman was often with soldiers when they died. When they did, he occasionally wrote their families with the news or with more details. Although probably too long to be quoted in full, I will because these letters reveal a great deal about Whitman and his service during the war. In May of 1865, for example, a Pennsylvania soldier, Frank H. Irwin, died, and Whitman wrote his mother not long after:

Dear Madam: No doubt you and Frank's friends have heard the sad fact of his death in Hospital here, through his uncle, or the lady from Baltimore, who took his things. (I have not seen them, only heard of them visiting Frank.) I will write you a few lines— as a casual friend that sat by his death bed.

Your son, Corporal Frank H. Irwin, was wounded near Fort Fisher, Virginia, March 25th, 1865—the wound was in the left knee, pretty bad. He was sent up to Washington, was receiv'd in Ward C, Armory Square Hospital, March 28th—the wound became worse, and on the 4th of April the leg was amputated a little above the knee—the operation was performed by Dr. Bliss, one of the best surgeons in the army—he did the whole operation himself—there was a good deal of bad matter gather'd—the bullet was found in the knee. For a couple of weeks afterwards he was doing pretty well. I visited and sat by him frequently, as he was fond of having me. The last ten or twelve days of April I saw that his case was critical. He previously had some fever, with cold spells. The last week in April he was much of the time flighty—but always mild and gentle. He died first of May. The actual cause of death was Pyaemia, (the absorption of the matter in the system instead of its discharge.)

Frank, as far as I saw, had everything requisite in surgical treatment, nursing, & c. He had watches much of the time. He was so good and well-behaved, and affectionate, I myself liked him very much. I was in the habit of coming in afternoons and sitting by him, and soothing him, and he liked to have me—liked to put his arm out and lay his hand on my knee—would keep it so a long while. Toward the last he was more restless and flighty at night—often fancied himself with his regiment—by his talk sometimes seem'd as if his feelings were hurt by being blamed by his officers for something he was entirely innocent of—said, "I never in my life was thought capable of such a thing, and never was." At other times he would fancy himself talking as it seem'd to children or such like, his relatives I suppose, and giving them good advice; would talk to them a long while. All the time he was out of his head not one single bad word or thought or idea escaped him. It was remark'd that many a man's conversation in his sense was not half as good as Frank's delirium.

He was perfectly willing to die—he had become very weak and had suffer'd a good deal, and was perfectly resign'd, poor boy. I do not know his past life, but I feel as if it must have been good. At any rate what I saw of him here, under the most trying circumstances, with a painful wound, and among strangers, I can say that he behaved so brave, so composed, and so sweet and affectionate, it could not be surpass'd. And now like many other noble and good men, after serving his country as a soldier, he has yielded up his young life at the very outset in her service. Such things are gloomy—yet there is a text, "God doeth all things well,"—the meaning of which, after due time, appears to the soul.

I thought perhaps a few words, though from a stranger, about your son, from one who was with him at the last, might be worth while, for I loved the young man, though I but saw him immediately to lose him. I am merely a friend visiting the Hospitals occasionally to cheer the wounded and sick.[66]

I have stopped reading this letter aloud in class when I teach Whitman because I do not trust myself to make it through without tearing up, especially if I did not get much sleep the night before, which, for some reason, makes the tears flow more freely. What gets me is how profoundly and thoroughly *decent* Whitman is in reporting the death of this soldier to the soldier's mother. Whitman does not spare—or does not seem to—any of the details of the son's wounds. He "had suffer'd a good deal," Whitman admits. Yet he also assures Mrs. Irwin that her son received the best care, and that everything that could be done for him was done for him. Crucially, Whitman does not ignore the tragedy of his death. But he also provides Irwin's mother with a text, "God doeth all things well," which, though he might not believe it, nevertheless might comfort her. The passage from Scripture also reassures Irwin's mother that her son died for a purpose.

Whitman does not specify which purpose, whether defending the Union or abolishing slavery, but the purpose was part of God's plan. In any case, her son did not die in vain. Whitman also testifies to what I imagine every mother would want to hear of her son; namely, that he was, even in his delirium, a good person. Finally, and perhaps most important, Whitman reassures Irwin's mother that her son did not die alone. Someone "who loved the young man"—Whitman—"sat by his death bed" and "was with him at the last."

The letter is more than "worth while," as Whitman puts it. Under the circumstances, you could not ask for a better letter. You believe Whitman when he says that he loved the young man, and his love almost makes the death of the young man bearable. If I had a son who died far away from me, I would want to know just the things that Whitman writes, and I would be eternally grateful that someone like Whitman was with him when he died.

VII.

After reading Whitman's *Memoranda During the War*, his diary-like accounting of his Civil War years, most people come away feeling as I do, which is overcome by, perhaps slightly in awe of, Whitman's fundamental human decency. In his First Inaugural Address, Whitman's political hero, Abraham Lincoln, spoke of the better angels of our nature. To me, Whitman is the incarnation of that better angel.

The question, however, is what any of this has to do with democracy. Whitman's service to soldiers during the Civil War may have been admirable, even saintly, but it does not seem political in any ordinary sense of the term. Yet Whitman certainly thought of his hospital work as a matter of democracy, and the answer as to how or why lies, I think, in his letter to the mother of Corporal Frank H. Irwin. Although he admits that he did not know the soldier's past life, Whitman nevertheless concludes that Irwin "must have been good." Whitman drew the same conclusion about most if not all of the young men he visited during the Civil War, and he rejoiced in the discovery and what it meant for the United States. "I now doubt whether one can get a fair sense of what this War practically is," he wrote early in the Civil War, "or what genuine America is, and her character, without some such experience as this I am having."[67] Fatefully, his experience confirmed his intuitions about what he elsewhere called "the divine average," the common man.

While once again visiting the front in Culpeper, Virginia, in February of 1864, Whitman awoke in the middle of the night to watch a line of soldiers marching back from a deployment. "It may have been odd," Whitman remarked of the experience, "but I never before so realized the majesty and reality of the American common people proper. It fell upon me like a great awe."[68] "Before I went down to the Field and among the Hospitals," Whitman admits in *Memoranda During the War*, "I had my hours of doubt about These States; but not since. . . . Curious as it may seem, the War, to me, *proved* Humanity, and proved America and the Modern."[69] The hospitals propped up his faith in the common man when everything else seemed to erode such faith. "Let no tongue ever speak in disparagement of the American races, north or south," he writes in *Democratic Vistas*, rebuking critics of democracy like Thomas Carlyle and even himself, "to one who has been through the war in the great army hospitals."[70] With young men like Corporal Irwin, Whitman thought, democracy could not go wrong.

Specifically, Irwin and other soldiers displayed the character and the virtues that Whitman thought necessary to a democracy.

After having been in the hospitals for only a few weeks, Whitman wrote Ralph Waldo Emerson that "I find the masses fully justified by close contact, never vulgar, ever calm, without greediness, no flummery, no frivolity—responding electric and without fail to affection, yet no whining—not the first unmanly whimper have I yet seen or heard."[71] And, as we have seen, Whitman wrote Irwin's mother that "under the most trying circumstances, with a painful wound, and among strangers, I can say that he [Irwin] behaved so brave, so composed, and so sweet and affectionate." As these passages suggest, Whitman admired soldiers for their courage and their willingness, including those who fought for the South, to sacrifice their lives for an abstraction like freedom or union or sovereignty. By contrast, in his darker moments, he feared that most Americans thought first and foremost of their material interests, of their property, their money, and their lives, which they would never sacrifice to something as immaterial and profitless as an idea. Soldiers, however, proved him wrong. They, as he put it, *proved* humanity.

Whitman also admired how stoically and courageously soldiers accepted death. In his letter to Emerson, he relates that the chief surgeon in the Patent Office Hospital "told me last evening that he had not in memory one single case of a man's meeting the approach of death, whether sudden or slow, with fear or trembling—but always of these young men meeting their death with steady composure, and often with curious readiness."[72] For someone who had previously written that "to die is different from what anyone supposed, and luckier," this news of soldiers composedly and readily meeting death must have warmed his heart.

In short, the soldiers whom Whitman encountered during the war seemed to embody each of the virtues he had tried to reflect—and inspire—through his poems. In doing so, they renewed his faith in the possibilities of democracy in the United States.

Perhaps the most constant and enthusiastic refrain in his descriptions of soldiers, though, is how they respond to and offer affection. In his letter to Irwin's mother, he mentions it twice. Irwin was "affectionate" and "so sweet and affectionate." In his letter to Emerson, the masses respond "electric and without fail to affection." (This from the author of a poem titled "I Sing the Body Electric.") Moreover, it—affection—is the subject of Whitman's greatest Civil War poem, "Vigil Strange I Kept on the Field One Night." The poem is spoken by a soldier who watches a fellow soldier die in battle at his side. (The speaker of the poem refers to this fellow soldier as "my son and my comrade," which suggests that the two may be father and son, but elsewhere "son" is used metaphorically, so their relationship is not entirely clear.) Because he must continue onward in battle the living soldier can only pause to exchange a meaningful look with his dying comrade and to touch his outstretched hand. That night, however, the soldier returns to keep vigil over the body of the fallen soldier, and his address to him is heartbreaking:

> Found you in death so cold, dear comrade—found your
>   body, son of responding kisses (never again on earth
>   responding);
> Bared your face in the starlight—curious the scene—cool blew
>   the moderate night-wind;
> Long there and then in vigil I stood, dimly around me the
>   battle-field spreading;
> Vigil wondrous and vigil sweet, there in the fragrant
>   silent night;
> . . . .
> Vigil of silence, love and death—vigil for you, my son
>   and my soldier,
> As onward silently stars aloft, eastward new ones upward stole;

Vigil final for you, brave boy (I could not save you, swift was
   your death,
I faithfully loved you and cared for you living—I think we shall
   surely meet again);
Till at latest lingering of the night, indeed just as the
   dawn appear'd,
My comrade I wrapt in his blanket, envelop'd well his form,
Folded the blanket well, tucking it carefully over head, and
   carefully under feet;
And there and then, and bathed by the rising sun, my son in
   his grave, in his rude-dug grave I deposited;
Ending my vigil strange with that—vigil of night and battle-
   field dim;
Vigil for boy of responding kisses (never again on earth
   responding);
Vigil for comrade swiftly slain—vigil I never forget, how as
   day brighten'd,
I rose from the chill ground, and folded my soldier well
   in his blanket,
And buried him where he fell.[73]

You can detect a bit of Whitman in the older man who keeps
vigil over the dead body of a younger man. After all, Whitman
did it many times in the hospitals. Yet Whitman also admired
the affection he witnessed between soldiers, which the poem
tenderly portrays. Notice how the speaker repeats himself, over
and over, repeats exact phrases, in fact, which suggests that he
is unwilling or unable to move on from the death. Just as he was
forced to leave his comrade only to return to him later, his speech
leaves a phrase only to return to it later. Notice, too, the care
with which the speaker buries the body. The metaphor is of seal-
ing and sending a letter. His form is "envelop'd," the blanket is

tucked carefully over head and carefully under feet, and his body is "deposited" in the rude-dug grave, just as a letter is deposited in a mailbox. The comrade is being buried in the ground, but like a letter he is also being sent someplace, somewhere, the speaker believes, where they "shall surely meet again."

To my way of reading it, the most striking aspect of the poem is its syntax, which might seem like an odd thing to say, but once you see it, it makes sense. Most sentences have a subject-verb-object structure. "I read the book." "Stars stole upward." "I buried the body." But notice that Whitman consistently alters conventional syntax. Sentences do not proceed subject-verb-object but, usually, and somewhat awkwardly, object-subject-verb. Look at the title: "Vigil Strange I Kept on the Field One Night." Usually, one would just say "I kept a strange vigil on the field one night." Instead, Whitman puts object (vigil) before subject (I) and verb (kept). Or later in the poem, instead of writing "I wrapt my comrade in his blanket," he writes, "My comrade I wrapt in his blanket." The shift, I believe, makes Whitman's point about affection. Instead of occupying the position of authority, boldly commanding the world and its objects, as subjects usually do in sentences, the subject in the sentences of Whitman's poem subordinates itself to the object. It serves them, just as—and here is the crucial part—the speaker subordinates himself to his object, his comrade. The form of the sentences reflects the content of the poem. Grammar becomes ethics. In both poem and syntax, what matters is not the self but the self in relation to someone or something else. At the end of the poem, normal syntax returns, almost as though once the body is in the ground the speaker needs to reassert himself as a subject. But the return to normal syntax only highlights how strange the earlier variations really are.

So what Whitman says matters, but so does how he says it. Both contribute to what I believe Whitman means by affection, manly love, adhesiveness, comradeliness, and what makes that virtue by whatever name so crucial to his notion of democracy. In affectionate relationships, you subordinate yourself to others. You put their interests above your own. Or, to put it another way, you make their interests your own. In short, you care about and for them. That is what Whitman did for soldiers, and that, in "Vigil Strange I Kept on the Field One Night," is what soldiers did for each other.

For Whitman, that affection, and only that sort of affection, would form the basis of any democracy worth the name.

As discussed in the chapter on Whitman's sexuality, around the same time that he published *Democratic Vistas*, he wrote: "In my opinion, it is by a fervent, accepted development of comradeship, the beautiful and sane affection of man for man, latent in all the young fellows, north and south, east and west—it is by this, I say, and by what goes directly and indirectly along with it, that the United States of the future, (I cannot too often repeat,) are to be most effectually welded together, intercalated, anneal'd into a living union."[74] "Manly friendship," he elsewhere observed, would have "the deepest relation to general politics."[75]

This is all well and good, but what would a democracy founded on affection look like? At a very basic level, it implies a robust welfare state. In order to survive, human beings need food, shelter, clothing, warmth, and medical care. When individuals cannot, or even will not, supply those needs for themselves, we, through the mediation of the state, must supply them. Needs, the philosopher Michael Ignatieff has written, make rights, and the welfare state exists to meet those needs and honor those rights.

Yet, as Ignatieff recognizes, our needs as human beings exceed those things (food, shelter, and clothing) that merely allow us to survive. In order to flourish, we need other, less tangible things: fraternity, love, belonging, dignity, and respect. A welfare state frees each of us from charity, whether providing it or taking it. It therefore serves the needs of freedom. It does not, however, or only very indirectly, serve the needs of comradeship. Even under the most robust and generous welfare state, a society can remain a society of strangers.[76] Above all, Whitman wanted to transcend that society of strangers. He did not want the state to look out for us (he lived before very many people even thought of that as a possibility), but wanted each of us to look out for the other. Or, to put it slightly differently, the state could meet some of our needs, but only comrades could meet our last and most important needs.

Consider what Whitman did and did not do for sick and wounded soldiers in the Civil War hospitals. As well as could be expected, their material needs—food, housing, medical care— were provided for by the state. What Whitman offered soldiers, by contrast, was something less yet also something more. By writing letters for them, by finding them something to read, by giving them spending money, by sitting by their side when they were frightened and alone, Whitman treated soldiers with dignity and respect. He loved them, and they loved him back. We have difficulty speaking of, say, the need for love as a right, but those unspeakable needs do not matter any less because of that. The basic needs matter first, but the other needs matter equally, if that is not too oxymoronic. Think about the corpse in "Vigil Strange I Kept on the Field One Night." It no longer needs to survive, yet it still deserves the dignity and respect offered by the surviving soldier.

Do not get me wrong. I would trade almost anything for a more robust welfare state than the one Americans currently pay for, and much in Whitman's poetry implies the need for one and thus the right to one. But a democracy—a nation—is more than a robust welfare state. You can, for example, define democracy in a minimal way. It exists to protect the rights of individuals, to give elected leaders the legitimacy needed to make decisions on our behalf, and to grant the electorate the right to throw the bums out, which will keep the bums honest, or honest enough, anyway. Or you can define democracy in a slightly larger way. Public discussion and the popular vote is a way for us to achieve the common good, including the common good that comes from closing the distance between the wealthy and everyone else. I think most of us, especially liberals, think of democracy in this slightly larger way, and say that it succeeds to the extent that individuals participate in it and problems get solved.

But it is possible to conceive, as Whitman does, of democracy larger still. For Whitman, democracy is a way of being; in particular, it is a way of being with others. From this perspective, democracy has relatively little to do with what Congress does, what the president promises to do, what laws the Supreme Court finds constitutional or unconstitutional, who you vote for or even whether you vote or not. Instead, it has much more to do with how you approach your fellow men and women. Do you respect them? Do you acknowledge their dignity? Do you identify your interests with theirs? In short, do you love them? Not all of them, of course, not even very many, really, but enough of them that everyone is included in the chain of affection, enough so that no one gets left out. If you do, and if you are so loved, Whitman believes, then, politically speaking, everything else will take care of itself.[77]

In "Over the Carnage Rose Prophetic a Voice," a poem written before the Civil War but altered afterward, Whitman writes, "Be not dishearten'd, affection shall solve the problems of freedom yet."[78] Fittingly, the poem began life as one of the "Calamus" poems, those pre–Civil War poems devoted to manly love, but in later editions Whitman included it in the Drum-Taps section, his poems about the Civil War. For Whitman, democracy requires affection, and affection alone would bring about true democracy.

Sounds good, you might think, but realistically, do Americans have such affection in them today? Would a visit to the wards of a Veterans Hospital and conversations with the casualties of our own wars make us feel better about our fellow Americans or the appalling spectacle that is democracy in the United States today? I have my doubts, but not fully. Of course, I do not expect universal love to triumph any time soon, and a trip to the mall can still stoke my doubts about the common man. Tragically, too, Americans' homophobia may have undone much of the capacity for affection to which Whitman looked to save democracy.

Even so, at bottom, I think we do care about each other, not always, and not consistently, but sometimes. In which case, we might well believe that the spectacle of democracy is as appalling to us as it was to Whitman, and perhaps that it will be appalling for the foreseeable future. But we might also draw comfort from the fact that, thanks in part to Whitman, we know where democracy in the United States must head: toward affection, toward friendship, toward a nation founded on care. I do not know how, or even whether, we as a country can get there, but I am daily grateful to Whitman for offering such a clear and compelling vision of where we must head. We might also draw comfort, as Whitman did, from the fact that though much of our politics and culture conspires against it, somewhere within them Americans have sufficient reserves of affection to get us there.

At Whitman's Tomb

Who has done his day's work and will soonest be
through with his supper?
Who wishes to walk with me?
—WALT WHITMAN, "Song of Myself" (1855)

I love Walt Whitman. I hate Walt Whitman's tomb.
A few months shy of his seventy-third birthday, Whitman died on March 26 in 1892. He died from so many different maladies—pleurisy, consumption, tuberculosis, nephritis—that no single cause of death could take credit. At his funeral, seemingly all of Camden turned out. Thousands streamed through his Mickle Street house to view his body. Just as many joined the procession of Whitman's coffin to nearby Harleigh Cemetery, where the poet was laid to rest in a stone mausoleum along with the bodies of his mother and his father and, eventually, those of his sister Hannah, his brothers Edward and George, and George's wife, Hannah.[1]

When I visited Camden to tour Whitman's house, I made the drive down Haddon Avenue, one of the grimmest stretches of road in all of America, to Whitman's tomb at Harleigh Cemetery. After the boarded-up, post-apocalyptic streets of Camden, Harleigh Cemetery can seem like Eden. The cemetery lolls over

Whitman's tomb on the day of his burial, 1892

130 acres and sits next to the Cooper River Lake. After a morning of nothing but rain, the sun came out, and everything glistened.

Whitman's tomb lies at the far end of a small circle drive. A short gravel pathway leads to it. Two oak trees stand guard. Whitman designed the tomb himself, after an etching, *Death's Door*, by William Blake for Robert Blair's 1743 poem "The Grave." Blake's etching is stirring. As an actual tomb, though, it does not work nearly so well. Its pitched roof is about the height of its supporting pillars, making it seem squat. It looks like a troll might live inside.

There are as well other reasons to dislike it. The tomb cost Whitman a small fortune, twice as much as his house on Mickle Street, and it would have nearly bankrupted him if a friend had not stepped in and paid the remainder of the bill.[2] Whether it cost a lot or a little, the tomb seems ostentatious, even belabored, and, for Whitman anyway, deeply out of character. In the closing lines of "Song of Myself," he had already described the perfect grave for his body:

> I bequeath myself to the dirt to grow from the grass I love,
> If you want me again look for me under your bootsoles.[3]

Instead of letting you think of Whitman and his atoms circulating everywhere, the tomb at Harleigh Cemetery confines him to a single, very much fixed place. Far better for Whitman to have been deposited, as the dead soldier in his touching Civil War poem "Vigil Strange I Kept on the Field One Night" is, in a rude-dug grave with a plain or even no headstone. Then you could more easily imagine him bequeathed to the dirt and growing from the grass he loved, or more easily find him there under your bootsoles.

In addition to fixing him to one place, the tomb suggests all the wrong things about death, at least as Whitman viewed death. The tomb seems too solid, too designed to outlast the vulnerable, rotting bodies within it. It implies that death is something to be resisted or even undone, when Whitman had insisted on just the opposite. Death was not the end of life but the beginning. "To die," he writes in "Song of Myself,"

Death's Door *by William Blake*

"is different from what anyone supposed, and luckier."[4] There is nothing lucky about death in Whitman's tomb.

To be sure, if you read the poem from which Whitman cribbed the design for his tomb, Robert Blair's "The Grave," the mausoleum seems slightly less offensive. Although Blair spends pages painting "the gloomy horrors of the tomb," in the conclusion of the poem—where Blake's etching appears—Blair compares the grave to a bed, from which, he writes, we arise in the morning and fly away.[5] Hence Blake's etching, which shows an old man being hurried through death's door and into the utter darkness of the grave. Atop the door, though, sits the rejuvenated man, what the aged man will become in his next life. Death's Door, that is, leads onward to life.

But most people who visit Whitman's tomb will not know Blake's etching or Blair's poem. To them, Whitman's tomb will seem to lead nowhere. No figure of the renovated man sits atop the tomb to indicate the life to come. Instead, the tomb will seem like a hedge against time and decay. It will seem like *Death's Door* leads to death, full stop, and the only thing that remains of you is what you leave behind. That may be a more accurate view of death, but it was not Blair's view of death and it was certainly not Whitman's.

Of course, Whitman had his reasons for his tomb, and we should probably be more generous to him. He no doubt wanted to leave behind a monument, someplace where people could gather and memorialize him, and he seems to have wanted to gather the bodies of his scattered family in one place, all of which is fair enough. Grant a dying man his wish.

Still, it feels like Whitman missed a chance with his tomb, and so when I think of his legacy, I prefer a far different one to the slightly grandiose and misleading monument to himself. Coincidentally, that legacy begins with someone buried in

Whitman's tomb, his brother George, or, rather, George's son, Walter Orr Whitman. In 1875, George and his wife, Louisa, named their first-born son after Walt, who lived with the couple in Camden when Walter Orr Whitman was born. Alas, Walt's namesake only lived eight months.[6] Nevertheless, Walter Orr Whitman would be the first of many sons named after the poet.

During the Civil War, in the Armory Square Hospital, Whitman nursed a soldier from Syracuse, New York, named Benton H. Wilson. After the war, Wilson went home, married, and kept up an intermittent correspondence with Whitman. In 1868, Wilson wrote to say "My little baby Walt is well & Bright as a new dollar."[7] Another soldier, William H. Millis, from Delaware, whom the poet also nursed back to health during the war, wrote in 1875 that he and his wife "have had a son borned since we heard from you & We call him Walter Whitman Millis in honer [*sic*] to you for Love for you."[8] In 1887, an Alabama cotton farmer and Whitman enthusiast named John Newton Johnson arrived in Camden with a twelve-year-old boy named Walt Whitman.[9] A few years later, Henry Fritzinger, who had been raised by Whitman's Camden housekeeper and companion, Mary Davis, and whose brother, Warren, was Whitman's nurse during his declining years, named his son Walter Whitman Fritzinger.[10] Perhaps the most famous of the Whitman namesakes is the development economist Walter Whitman Rostow, born in 1916 to socialist parents who had emigrated from Russia. (Walter Whitman Rostow had two brothers: Eugene Debs Rostow and Ralph Waldo Emerson Rostow.)[11]

My favorite Whitman namesake, though, has to be Walter Whitman Odets, son of the playwright Clifford Odets, best known for his 1935 play *Waiting for Lefty*, the great one-act rabble-rouser. In 1952, like others who had flirted with the Communist Party during the Great Depression, Odets was summoned before

the House Un-American Activities Committee. On the train to
the hearings in Washington, he jotted some notes for his testi-
mony on the back of an envelope. He wrote: "No committee is
going to tell me, who named his son after America's greatest poet,
what it means to be an American."[12]

Since beginning this book, I have kept a running list of
Whitman namesakes. These are just the ones I found. Doubtless
many more Walts and Walter Whitmans have lived and died or
are living still.

It may seem obvious why a parent would name their child
after someone they know or think highly of, but there is more
to it than at first glance. Some parents may hope that by naming
a child after someone they respect, some of the qualities that
inhere to that person may adhere to their namesake. But ordi-
narily parents simply name their child after someone whom they
admire. (Walt Whitman's father named his other sons Andrew
Jackson Whitman, Thomas Jefferson Whitman, and George
Washington Whitman.) Despite his non-standard spelling, the
soldier William H. Millis may have put it best. Millis and his wife
named their child Walt, as Millis put it to Whitman, "In honer to
you for Love for you."

With Whitman, you can imagine why so many would honor,
love, feel grateful toward, and ultimately name their children after
him. For soldiers like Wilson and Millis, Whitman had nursed
them back to health. They owed him their lives, and they tried
to repay that debt by naming their son after him. But the same
applies to those who did not know Whitman or only knew him
through his poetry, like Clifford Odets or the parents of Walt
Whitman Rostow. They, too, may have felt as if they owed their
lives to Whitman. They, too, found themselves in Whitman's debt.

Ralph Waldo Emerson recognized this debt to Whitman
almost immediately. In his 1855 letter to Whitman thanking him

for sending him the first edition of *Leaves of Grass*, Emerson wrote, "I find incomparable things said incomparably well" and, in the last sentence of the letter, fittingly referred to Whitman as his "benefactor."[13] When Emerson read him, Whitman was on his way to becoming, as Odets put it on the back of his envelope, America's greatest poet, and we inevitably feel a debt toward that poet for his gift to us. "When we are moved by art," Lewis Hyde writes in his occasionally fuzzyheaded but often insightful classic *The Gift*, "we are grateful that the artist lived, grateful that he labored in the service of his gifts."[14] In recompense, we offer the name of our child, even if the poet is no longer around to receive the honor.

To me, that is Whitman's legacy, far more than his squat, overpriced tomb. "Anything I have I bestow," Whitman writes in "Song of Myself," and we recognize the gift Whitman bestowed on us.[15] Whitman—and the poetry he wrote—help us live. He lessens our burden. He makes dying easier. He puts money in its place. He teaches us to exalt our bodies. He restores our faith in democracy. He gives us ways to view the world when our existing ways feel exhausted, feel dead. When we suffer from malaise, he is good health to us.

After reading him, after absorbing him, we too feel like we owe him our lives, feel like we are in his debt. As best we can, we repay him. We name our son after him; we write books about him; or best of all, we keep attending to what he has to say.

Notes

INTRODUCTION: WALT WHITMAN—A POETIC COMFORT

Epigraph: Walt Whitman, "Preface" in *Leaves of Grass* (1855; repr., New York: Library of America, 1982), 24.

1. Kevin Mattson, *"What the Heck Are You Up To, Mr. President?": Jimmy Carter, America's "Malaise," and the Speech that Should Have Changed the Country* (New York: Bloomsbury, 2009).

2. Daniel Dale, "The Worst Speech of All Time," *Toronto Star*, July 19, 2009, http://www.thestar.com/news/insight/2009/07/19/the_worst_speech_of_all_time.html.

3. True, as of June 2014, the unemployment rate had fallen to 6.1 percent from a high of 10 percent in October of 2009, but most of the decline has occurred not because the unemployed have found jobs but because they have stopped looking for them. As a result, they no longer count as unemployed. The labor participation rate, the number of workers age sixteen and over who have a job, fell from a high of 66 percent in October 2008 to a low of 62.8 percent in December 2013, where it has settled since. For the unemployment rate, see Bureau of Labor Statistics, "Unemployment Rate," http://data.bls.gov/timeseries/LNS14000000; for the labor employment rate, see Bureau of Labor Statistics, "Labor Force Participation Rate," http://data.bls.gov/timeseries/LNS11300000; on child poverty, see U.S. Census Bureau, "Poverty Status by Age, Race, and Hispanic Origin," Historical Poverty Tables, Table 3, http://www.census.gov/hhes/www/poverty/data/historical/people.html.

4. Emmanuel Saez, "Striking It Richer: The Evolution of Top Incomes in the United States" (updated with 2009 and 2010 estimates), http://elsa.berkeley.edu/~saez/saez-UStopincomes-2010.pdf.

5. Rasmussen Reports, "Just 15% Think Today's Children Will Be Better Off than Their Parents," February 5, 2013, http://www.rasmussenreports.com/public_content/business/general_business/january_2013/just_15_think_today_s_children_will_be_better_off_than_their_parents.

6. U.S. Census Bureau, "Selected Economic Characteristics," http://factfinder2.census.gov/faces/tableservices/jsf/pages/productview.xhtml?pid=ACS_12_5YR_DP03.

7. Laura Ly, "State of New Jersey Stepping in to Run Camden's Troubled Schools," CNN.com, March 25, 2013, http://www.cnn.com/2013/03/25/us/new-jersey-camden-schools/.

8. Deborah Hirsch, "Report Ranks Camden Most Dangerous City in U.S.," *Courier-Post*, November 24, 2009, http://www.courierpostonline.com/article/20091124/NEWS01/911240338/Report-ranks-Camden-most-dangerous-U-S-city; Joseph Goldstein, "Police Force Nearly Halved, Camden Feels Impact," *New York Times*, March 6, 2011, http://www.nytimes.com/2011/03/07/nyregion/07camden.html?pagewanted=all; "Camden No. 1 Again . . . ," *Philly.com*, January 13, 2013, http://www.philly.com/philly/blogs/camden_flow/188927931.html; Chris Hedges, "City of Ruins," *The Nation*, September 4, 2010, http://www.the-nation.com/article/155801/city-ruins#; "New Jersey Woman Beheads Her Son, 2," *New York Times*, August 22, 2012, http://www.nytimes.com/2012/08/23/nyregion/camden-nj-woman-decapitates-her-toddler.html; "Man Arrested in Grisly Attack on Two Siblings in New Jersey," *New York Times*, September 3, 2012, http://www.nytimes.com/2012/09/04/nyregion/man-arrested-in-grisly-attack-on-siblings-in-new-jersey.html.

9. See Jefferson Cowie, *Capital Moves: RCA's Seventy-Year Quest for Cheap Labor* (New York: New Press, 2001).

10. Whitman, "A Song for Occupations," in *Leaves of Grass*, 89.

11. For biographical information on Whitman, I relied on two books: Justin Kaplan, *Walt Whitman: A Life* (New York: Simon and Schuster, 1980); and, more often, David Reynolds, *Walt Whitman's America: A Cultural Biography* (New York: Vintage Books, 1995).

12. Whitman, "Song of Myself," in *Leaves of Grass*, 27. Here and elsewhere, unless otherwise indicated, ellipses like those in the final quoted line are Whitman's and should not be read as omitted text.

13. Ibid., 29.

14. "Whitman's Leaves of Grass," *Putnam's Monthly: A Magazine of Literature, Science, and Art*, September 1855, 321.

15. See Michael Robertson, *Worshipping Walt: The Whitman Disciples* (Princeton: Princeton University Press, 2008).

16. Oscar Wilde to Walt Whitman, 1 March 1882, in *The Letters of Oscar Wilde*, ed. Rupert Hart-Davis (New York: Harcourt, Brace & World, 1962), 100.

17. Ralph Waldo Emerson to Walter Whitman, 21 July 1855, in *The Letters of Ralph Waldo Emerson*, vol. 8 (New York: Columbia University Press, 1991), 446.

18. William James, *The Varieties of Religious Experience* (1902; repr., New York: Touchstone, 2004), 64.

19. Herman Melville to Nathaniel Hawthorne, April 1851, vol. 14: *Correspondence*, in *The Writings of Herman Melville* (Evanston, IL:

Northwestern University Press, 1993), 186.

20.   Whitman, "To Think of Time," in *Leaves of Grass* (1891–92; repr., New York: Library of America, 1982), 557; James, *Varieties of Religious Experience*, 67.

21.   Chris Hedges, *Empire of Illusion: The End of Literacy and the Triumph of Spectacle* (New York: Nation Books, 2009), 49.

22.   Whitman, "Song of Myself," 58.

23.   Horace Traubel, *With Walt Whitman in Camden*, vol. 7 (Carbondale: Southern Illinois University Press, 1992), 386.

24.   Whitman, "Preface," 26.

25.   Whitman, "Song of Myself," 88.

CHAPTER 1: CONGRATULATIONS! YOU'RE DEAD!

Epigraph: Walt Whitman, "Song of Myself," *Leaves of Grass* (1855; repr., New York: Library of America, 1982), 73.

1.   Tertullian, "The Apology," *The Ante-Nicene Fathers*, ed. Alexander Roberts, James Donaldson, Arthur Cleveland Coxe (New York: Cosimo Books, 2007), 3:43.

2.   Jon M. Sweeney, *Almost Catholic: An Appreciation of the History, Practice, & Mystery of Ancient Faith* (San Francisco: Jossey-Bass, 2004), 94.

3.   Philip Larkin, "Aubade," in *Collected Poems*, ed. Anthony Thwaite (New York: Farrar, Straus and Giroux, 2004), 190.

4.   Whitman, "Song of Myself," 32.

5.   Walt Whitman, *Specimen Days* (1882; repr., New York: Library of America, 1982), 700–701.

6.   Christopher Gray, "From Ghost Town to Park Gateway," *New York Times*, May 20, 2007, http://www.nytimes.com/2007/05/20/realestate/20scap.html; Michael M. Grynbaum and Adriane Quinlan, "East River Ferry Service, With 7 Stops, Starts Run," June 13, 2011, http://www.nytimes.com/2011/06/14/nyregion/east-river-ferry-service-begins-with-7-stops.html.

7.   Walt Whitman, "Crossing Brooklyn Ferry," in *Selected Poems 1855–1892: A New Edition*, ed. Gary Schmidgall (New York: St. Martin's Press, 1999), 135–36.

8.   Ibid., 135.

9.   Ibid., 134.

10.   Ibid., 135.

11.   Ibid.

12.   Ibid.

13. Ibid., 137.

14. Ibid., 138.

15. Ibid.

16. Ibid.

17. Ibid.

18. Ibid., 139–40.

19. See Brian Clegg, *Gravity: How the Weakest Force in the Universe Shaped Our Lives* (New York: St. Martin's Press, 2012).

20. Walt Whitman, *Notebooks and Unpublished Prose Manuscripts*, vol. 1: *The Collected Writings of Walt Whitman* (New York: New York University Press, 1984), 136.

21. Whitman, "Song of Myself," 46.

22. Ibid., 28.

23. Ibid., 46.

24. Whitman, "A Song for Occupations," *Leaves*, 92.

25. Robin Collins, "The Fine-Tuning Argument," *Readings in the Philosophy of Religion*, ed. Kelly James Clark (Peterborough, Ont.: Broadview Press, 2008), 84.

26. Holt, *Why Does the World Exist?*, 168.

27. Whitman, "Who Learns My Lesson Complete," in *Leaves of Grass*, 140.

28. Whitman, "Faith Poem," in *Selected Poems*, 153.

29. Whitman, "Song of Myself," 48.

30. Whitman, "Poem of Wonder at the Resurrection of the Wheat," in *Selected Poems*, 131.

31. Ibid.

32. Ibid., 132.

33. Whitman, "Song of Myself," 86.

34. Ibid., 31.

35. Ibid., 32.

36. Whitman, "Clef Poem," in *Selected Poems*, 151.

37. Whitman, "Song," 86.

38. Ibid., 78.

39. Ibid.

40. Ibid.

41. Ibid., 82.

42. Whitman, "Faith Poem," 154.

43. Whitman, "To One Shortly to Die," in *Leaves of Grass* (1892; repr., New York: Library of America, 1982), 565.

44. Whitman, "Song of Myself," 87.

45. Whitman, "Crossing Brooklyn Ferry," 137.

46. David S. Reynolds, *Walt Whitman* (New York: Oxford University Press, 2005), 242–43; Pierre-Simon Laplace, *The System of the World*, trans. J. Pond, vol. 2 (London: W. Flint, 1809).
47. Carl Sagan, *Cosmos: A Personal Voyage, Episode 1*, YouTube video, http://www.youtube.com/watch?v=ClPShKs9Kr0.
48. Whitman, "Crossing Brooklyn Ferry," 135.
49. Whitman, "Faith Poem," 153.
50. Whitman, "Song of Myself," 85, 57.
51. Whitman, "To Think of Time," *Leaves of Grass*, 106.
52. Ibid.
53. Whitman, "Crossing Brooklyn Ferry," 134.
54. Whitman, "Clef Poem," 151.

CHAPTER 2: WALT WHITMAN'S CREDIT REPORT LOOKS EVEN WORSE THAN YOURS

Epigraph: Walt Whitman, "A Song for Occupations," *Leaves of Grass* (1855; repr., New York: Library of America, 1982), 95.
1. Oral S. Coad, "Whitman vs. Parton," *Journal of the Rutgers University Library* 4 (1940): 1–8.
2. Horace Traubel, *With Walt Whitman in Camden*, vol. 1 (New York: Mitchell Kennerley, 1914), 235.
3. Ibid., vol. 3, 234–35.
4. Tamar Lewin, "Burden of College Loans on Graduates Grows," *New York Times*, April 11, 2011, http://www.nytimes.com/2011/04/12/education/12college.html.
5. Mary Pilon, "When Student Loans Live On After Death," *Wall Street Journal*, August 7, 2010, http://online.wsj.com/news/articles/SB10001424052748704741904575409510529783860.
6. Jordan Weissmann, "53% of Recent College Grads Are Jobless or Underemployed—How?" *The Atlantic*, April 23, 2012, http://www.theatlantic.com/business/archive/2012/04/53-of-recent-college-grads-are-jobless-or-underemployed-how/256237/.
7. Michael Kumhof and Romain Rancière, "Leveraging Inequality," *Finance & Development* 47/4 (2010), https://www.imf.org/external/pubs/ft/fandd/2010/12/kumhof.htm.
8. Tony Judt, with Timothy Snyder, *Thinking the Twentieth Century*, (New York: Penguin Press, 2012), 385.
9. Peter J. L. Riley, "Leaves of Grass and Real Estate," *Walt Whitman Quarterly Review* 28/4 (2011): 164–65.

10. Whitman, "Song of Myself," in *Leaves of Grass,* 38.
11. Walt Whitman, *The Gathering of the Forces,* ed. Cleveland Rodgers and John Black, vol. 2 (New York: G. P. Putnam's Sons, 1920), 64–83.
12. Leadie M. Clark, *Walt Whitman's Concept of the Common Man* (New York: Philosophical Library, 1955), 43.
13. Alexia Nader, "The Occupy Wall Street Library," *The New Yorker,* September 29, 2011, http://www.newyorker.com/online/blogs/books/2011/09/the-occupy-wall-street-library.html.
14. Whitman, "Song," 8.
15. Ibid., 9.
16. *The Uncollected Poetry and Prose of Walt Whitman,* ed. Emory Holloway, vol. 1 (Garden City, NY: Doubleday, Page, 1921), 124.
17. Whitman, "Song of Myself," 5.
18. Ibid., 6.
19. Ibid., 20.
20. Ibid., 20–21. Again, suspension points here and elsewhere are as in 1855 original. No words have been omitted.
21. Ibid., 21.
22. Ibid.
23. See David Dowling, *Capital Letters: Authorship in the Antebellum Literary Market* (Iowa City: Universty of Iowa Press, 2009).
24. Andrew Lawson, "'Spending for Vast Returns': Sex, Class, and Commerce in the First *Leaves of Grass,*" *American Literature* 75/2 (2003): 335–65.
25. Riley, "Leaves of Grass and Real Estate," 164.
26. Rachel Aviv, "Whitman *Really* Slept Here," *The Poetry Foundation,* October 18, 2006, http://www.poetryfoundation.org/article/178731.
27. Walt Whitman, *Democratic Vistas* (1871; repr., New York: Library of America, 1982), 937.
28. Walt Whitman, "The Tramp and the Strike Question," in *Complete Prose Works* (1892; repr., New York: Library of America, 1982), 1064.
29. Whitman, "Song of Myself," 23.
30. Ibid,, 21.
31. Matthew 16:26.
32. Whitman, "Song of Myself," 58.
33. Ibid., 27.
34. Traubel, *With Walt Whitman,* vol. 2, 445.
35. Frances Wright, *A Few Days in Athens* (Boston: J. P. Mendum, 1850), 177–78.
36. *Brooklyn Daily Eagle,* June 28, 1847, www.brooklynpubliclibrary.org/eagle.

37. Justus von Liebig, *Organic Chemistry in Its Application to Agriculture and Physiology* (London: Taylor & Walton, 1842), 262.
38. Whitman, "Song of Myself," 86.
39. Ibid., 31.
40. Holloway, *Uncollected Poetry and Prose of Walt Whitman,* vol. 1, 67–68.
41. Whitman, "Song," 23.
42. Ibid., 22.
43. Ibid.
44. Ibid.
45. Steve Sailer, "Q&A: Steven Pinker of 'Blank Slate,'" October 30, 2002, UPI, http://pinker.wjh.harvard.edu/books/tbs/media_articles/2002_10_30_upi.html.
46. Center for the Study of the American Dream, "Annual State of the American Dream Survey," http://www.xavier.edu/americandream/programs/survey.cfm.
47. Whitman, *Democratic Vistas* in *Complete Prose Works* (1892; repr., New York: Library of America, 1982), 951.
48. Rainer Maria Rilke, "Archaic Torso of Apollo," in *Selected Poems*, trans. Susan Ranson and Marielle Sutherland (New York: Oxford University Press, 2011), 83.
49. Whitman, "A Song for Occupations," 89.
50. Ibid., 90.
51. Ibid., 91.
52. Ibid., 92.
53. Ibid., 92–93.
54. Ibid., 98.
55. Ibid., 93.
56. Ibid., 93–94.
57. Ibid., 93.
58. Ibid., 98–99.
59. Robert J. Aalberts, *Real Estate Law*, 8th ed. (Mason, OH: South-Western Cengage Learning, 2012), 364–65.
60. Whitman, "Song of Myself," 27.
61. Bill Clinton and Albert Gore, *Putting People First: How We Can All Change America* (New York: Times Books, 1992).
62. Emmanuel Saez, "Striking It Richer: The Evolution of Top Incomes in the United States" (updated with 2009 and 2010 estimates), http://elsa.berkeley.edu/~saez/saez-UStopincomes-2010.pdf.
63. Ibid.

64. U.S. Census Bureau, "Census Bureau Reports Almost One in Three Americans Were Poor at Least Two Months from 2009 to 2011," January 7, 2014, http://www.census.gov/newsroom/releases/archives/poverty/cb14-05.html.

65. Motoko Rich, "Economic Insecurity," *New York Times*, November 22, 2011, http://economix.blogs.nytimes.com/2011/11/22/economic-insecurity/.

INTERLUDE: WAS WALT WHITMAN SOCIALIST?

Epigraph: Horace Traubel, *With Walt Whitman in Camden*, vol. 1 (Boston: Small, Maynard, 1906), 221.

1. Regionald A. Beckett, "Whitman as a Socialist Poet," *To-Day* (July 1888): 8–15.

2. Traubel, *With Walt Whitman*, vol. 2 (New York: Mitchell Kennerley, 1915), 4.

3. Ibid.

4. *American Dictionary of the English Language*, 3rd ed., "Socialism."

5. *Webster's New World College Dictionary*, 3rd ed., "Socialism."

6. W. H. Auden, "In Memory of W.B. Yeats," in *Collected Poems*, ed. Edward Mendelson (New York: Modern Library, 2007), 245.

7. Beckett, "Whitman as a Socialist Poet," 9.

8. Ibid., 11.

9. Ibid., 9.

10. Ibid., 10–11.

11. Ibid., 12.

12. See Isaiah Berlin, "Two Concepts of Liberty," in *Four Essays on Liberty* (New York: Oxford University Press, 1970).

13. Beckett, "Whitman as a Socialist Poet," 10.

14. Whitman, "Song of Myself" in *Leaves of Grass* (1855; repr. New York: Library of America, 1982), 50.

15. Newton Arvin, *Whitman* (New York: Macmillan, 1938), 252.

16. M. V. Ball, "Whitman and Socialism," in *Conserving Walt Whitman's Fame: Selections From Horace Traubel's "Conservator," 1890–1919*, ed. Gary Schmidgall (Iowa City: University of Iowa Press, 2006), 160–66.

17. Whitman, "Song of Myself," 50.

18. Arvin, *Whitman*, 264.

19. Ibid., 273.

20. Alec Waugh, "Rhys, Ernest Percival," *Oxford Dictionary of National Biography*, http://www.oxforddnb.com.

21. Traubel, *With Walt Whitman*, 1:221.
22. Ibid., 222.

CHAPTER 3: WITH WALT WHITMAN, MAKING IT RAIN

Epigraph: Horace Traubel, *With Walt Whitman in Camden*, vol. 3 (New York: Michell Kennerley, 1914), 452.

1. Walt Whitman, "Theory of a Cluster," in *Notebooks and Unpublished Prose Manuscripts*, ed. Edward F. Grier, vol. 1 (New York: New York University Press, 1984), 413.
2. Ibid.
3. Walt Whitman, "Native Moments," in *Selected Poems 1855–1892: A New Edition*, ed. Gary Schmidgall (New York: St. Martin's Press, 1999), 219.
4. David S. Reynolds, *Walt Whitman's America: A Cultural Biography* (New York: Vintage Books, 1995), 194.
5. Ibid., 540–41.
6. Walt Whitman, "A Memorandum at a Venture," in *Complete Prose Works* (1892; repr., New York: Library of America, 1982), 1031.
7. Traubel, *With Walt Whitman*, 3:452–53.
8. Ibid., 3:321.
9. Andrea Dworkin, "Pornography Is a Civil Rights Issue," in *Letters from a War Zone* (Brooklyn, NY: Lawrence Hills Books, 1993), 284.
10. Aristotle, *On Rhetoric*, trans. George A. Kennedy (New York: Oxford University Press, 1991), 144.
11. Ibid., 145.
12. Ibid., 144.
13. Ibid., 146–49.
14. Sigmund Freud, "On Narcissism: An Introduction," in *The Freud Reader*, ed. Peter Gay (New York: W. W. Norton, 1989), 558.
15. Ibid., 559–60.
16. M. Jimmie Killingsworth, *Walt Whitman's Poetry of the Body: Sexuality, Politics, and the Text* (Chapel Hill: University of North Carolina Press, 1989), 34.
17. Reynolds, *Walt Whitman's America*, 195.
18. Paul R. Abramson and Steven D. Pinkerton, *With Pleasure: Thoughts on the Nature of Human Sexuality* (New York: Oxford University Press, 1995), 121.
19. William Acton, *The Functions and Disorders of the Reproductive Organs*, 2nd ed. (Philadelphia: Lindsay and Blakiston, 1867), 144–45.
20. Ibid., 145.

21. Ibid.
22. Aristotle, *On Rhetoric*, 146.
23. Walt Whitman, "We Two, How Long We Were Fooled," in *Leaves of Grass* (1891–92; repr., New York: Library of America, 1982), 264.
24. Walt Whitman, "Song of Myself," in *Leaves of Grass* (1855; repr., New York: Library of America, 1982), 28.
25. Ibid., 50–51.
26. Ibid., 51.
27. Galations 5:16–17.
28. Whitman, "I Sing the Body Electric," in *Leaves of Grass*,122.
29. Ibid., 123.
30. Whitman, "Song of Myself," 27.
31. Ibid., 48.
32. Ibid., 29.
33. Whitman, "A Woman Waits for Me," in *Selected Poems*, 149.
34. Whitman, " I Sing the Body Electric," 120–21.
35. Laurie Abraham, "Teaching Good Sex," *New York Times*, November 16, 2011, http://www.nytimes.com/2011/11/20/magazine/teaching-good-sex.html.
36. Whitman, "We Two, How Long We Were Fooled," 265.
37. Acton, *Functions and Disorders*, 48–49.
38. Abramson and Pinkerton, *With Pleasure*, 173–74.
39. Walt Whitman, "Bunch Poem," in *Selected Poems*, 156–57.
40. Walt Whitman, "Crossing Brooklyn Ferry," in *Selected Poems,* 137.
41. See James C. Whorton, *Nature Cures: The History of Alternative Medicine in America* (New York: Oxford University Press, 2002), 87.
42. Whitman, "The Sleepers," in *Leaves of Grass*, 107.
43. Whitman, "A Memorandum," 1031.
44. "A Surgeon General's Untimely Candor," *New York Times*, December 10, 1994, http://www.nytimes.com/1994/12/10/opinion/a-surgeon-general-s-untimely-candor.html.
45. Jeffrey J. Kripal, *Esalen: America and the Religion of No Religion* (Chicago: University of Chicago Press, 2007), 164.
46. Chistopher Lasch, *The Culture of Narcissism: American Life in an Age of Diminishing Expectations* (New York: W. W. Norton, 1991), 12.
47. PBS, "Clinton, Chapter 1," *American Experience*, http://www.pbs.org/wgbh/americanexperience/features/bonus-video/clinton-chapter-1/.
48. Kenneth Starr, "The Starr Report," Part 3, *Washington Post*, 1998, http://www.washingtonpost.com/wp-srv/politics/special/clinton/icreport/icreport.htm.

49. Kenneth Starr, "The Starr Report," Part 2, *Washington Post*, 1998, http://www.washingtonpost.com/wp-srv/politics/special/clinton/icreport/icreport.htm.

50. Kenneth Starr, "The Starr Report," Part 1, *Washington Post*, 1998, http://www.washingtonpost.com/wp-srv/politics/special/clinton/icreport/icreport.htm.

INTERLUDE II: WAS WALT WHITMAN GAY?

1. Walt Whitman, "In Paths Untrodden" in *Selected Poems 1855–1892: A New Edition*, ed. Gary Schmidgall (New York: St. Martin's Press, 1999), 223.

2. James E. Miller, Jr., *Walt Whitman: An Encyclopedia*, "Calamus" (New York: Routledge, 1998), 97.

3. Walt Whitman, "When I Heard at the Close of Day," in *Selected Poems*, 234.

4. Walt Whitman, "Hours Continuing Long," in *Selected Poems*, 232–33.

5. Walt Whitman, "Who Is Now Reading This?," in *Selected Poems*, 237–38.

6. Whitman, "Hours Continuing Long," 232.

7. See Jerome Loving, "Emory Holloway and the Quest for Whitman's 'Manhood,'" *Walt Whitman Quarterly Review* 11/1 (1993), 12–14.

8. Hershel Parker, "The Real 'Live Oak, with Moss': Straight Talk About Whitman's 'Gay Manifesto,'" *Nineteenth Century Literature* 51/2 (1996), 157.

9. Horace Traubel, *With Walt Whitman in Camden*, ed. Sculley Bradley, vol. 3 (New York: Mitchell Kennerley, 1914), 298.

10. Walt Whitman to Moncure D. Conway, November 1, 1867, *The Correspondence: 1842–1867*, ed. Edwin Haviland Miller, vol. 1 (New York: New York University Press, 1961), 346–47.

11. Walt Whitman, "Song of Myself," in *Leaves of Grass* (1855; repr., New York: Library of America, 1982), 31.

12. Whitman, "Paths," 223.

13. Ibid.

14. Walt Whitman, "Not Heat Flames Up and Consumes," "Whoever You Are Holding Me Now In Hand," and "To a Stranger," in *Selected Poems*, 236, 226, 241.

15. Walt Whitman, "Roots and Leaves Themselves Alone," in *Selected Poems*, 235.

16. Walt Whitman, "I Hear It Was Charged against Me," in *Selected Poems*, 243.

17. "Leaves of Grass," *The Saturday Review*, July 7, 1860, http://www.whitmanarchive.org/criticism/reviews/leaves1860/anc.00044.html.

18. Jerome Loving, *Walt Whitman: The Song of Himself* (Berkeley: University of California Press, 1999), 414.

19. It could be, as one Whitman scholar has recently written, that "the subject of homosexuality was totally sealed to the American mind," but that is not entirely true. One disgusted reviewer (Rufus Griswold) of the 1855 edition of *Leaves of Grass* referred obliquely to *"Peccatum illud horribile, inter Christianos non nominandum"* (that horrible sin not to be named among Christians). Specifically, the Latin phrase referred to sodomy, which was not, it would seem, *totally* sealed to the American mind. On the subject of homosexuality and the American mind, see *Walt Whitman's Mystical Ethics of Comradeship: Homosexuality and the Marginality of Friendship at the Crossroads of Modernity* (Albany: State University of New York Press, 2010), 3. See Rufus W. Griswold, "Review of *Leaves of Grass* (1855)," *The Criterion*, November, 10, 1855, http://www.whitman-archive.org/criticism/reviews/leaves1855/anc.00016.html.

20. E. Anthony Rotundo, "Romantic Friendships: Male Intimacy and Middle-Class Youth in the Northern United States, 1800–1900," *Journal of Social History* 23 (1989): 1–125; Rotundo, *American Manhood: Transformations in Masculinity from the Revolution to the Modern Era* (New York: Basic Books, 1993); John Champagne, "Walt Whitman, Our Great Gay Poet?" *Journal of Homosexuality* 55/4 (2008): 648–64; Jonathan Katz, *Love Stories: Sex between Men before Homosexuality* (Chicago: University of Chicago Press, 2001).

21. Quoted in Rotundo, *American Manhood*, 81.

22. Ibid.

23. Ibid.

24. Ibid.

25. Rotundo, "Romantic Friendships," 10. See also Michel Foucault, *The History of Sexuality*, trans. Robert Hurley, vol. 1 (New York: Vintage Books, 1988).

26. Ralph Waldo Emerson, "Friendship," in *Essays and Lectures*, ed. Joel Porte (New York: Library of America, 1983), 343.

27. Jonathan Katz, *Gay American History: Lesbians and Gay Men in the U.S.A.: A Documentary History* (New York: Meridian, 1992), 456.

28. Rotundo, "Romantic Friendships," 12.

29. Rotundo, *American Manhood*, 82.

30. Orson S. Fowler and Lorenzo N Fowler, *New Illustrated Self-Instructor in Phrenology and Physiology* (New York: Fowler and Wells, 1859), 84.

31. Orson Squire Fowler, *Phrenology: Proved, Illustrated, and Applied* (New York: W. H. Colyer, 1837), 65.

32. David S. Reynolds, *Walt Whitman's America: A Cultural Biography* (New York: Alfred A. Knopf, 1995), 247.

33. Walt Whitman, "Fast Anchor'd Eternal O Love!," in *Selected Poems*, 249.

34. Walt Whitman, "Proto-Leaf," in *Selected Poems*, 188. In the 1867 and subsequent editions, Whitman changed the title to "Starting from Paumonok."

35. Walt Whitman, "So Long!," in *Selected Poems*, 265.

36. Walt Whitman, *Democratic Vistas* (1871; repr., New York: Library of America, 1982), 981–982.

37. Walt Whitman, *Leaves of Grass* (1856), 356, http://www.whitmanarchive.org/published/LG/1856/whole.html.

38. Walt Whitman, "Preface, 1876," in *Complete Prose* (1892; repr., New York: Library of America, 1982), 1011.

39. Whitman, "Calamus 5," in *Selected Poems*, 228–29.

40. John Addington Symonds to Walt Whitman, February 7, 1872, http://www.whitmanarchive.org/biography/correspondence/reconstruction/tei/loc.01961.html.

41. Walt Whitman to John Addington Symonds, August 19, 1890, in Miller, *The Correspondence*, vol. 5, 72–73.

42. Horace Traubel, *With Walt Whitman in Camden*, vol. 1 (Boston: Small, Maynard, 1906), 76–77.

43. M. Jimmie Killingsworth, *Whitman's Poetry of the Body: Sexuality, Politics, and the Text* (Chapel Hill: University of North Carolina Press, 1989), 167.

44. Walt Whitman, *The Uncollected Poetry and Prose of Walt* Whitman, ed. Emory Holloway, vol. 2 (Garden City, NY: Doubleday, Page, 1921), 96.

45. David Kuebrich, "Comradeship," in *Walt Whitman: An Encyclopedia*, ed. J. R. LeMaster and Donald D. Kummings (New York: Garland Publishing, 1998), 144.

46. Reynolds, *Walt Whitman's America*, 576.

47. Sigmund Freud, "Fragment of an Analysis of a Case of Hysteria ('Dora')," in *The Freud Reader*, ed. Peter Gay (New York: W. W. Norton, 1989), 198.

48. Ibid.

CHAPTER 4: AFFECTION SHALL SOLVE THE PROBLEMS OF FREEDOM

Epigraph: Walt Whitman, "Over the Carnage Rose a Voice Prophetic," in *Leaves of Grass* (1891–92; repr., New York: Library of America, 1982), 449. This poem originally appeared in the 1860 edition of *Leaves of Grass* in the "Calamus" sequence and was revised and retitled for the 1867 edition.

1. Walt Whitman to Thomas Jefferson Whitman, January 16, 1863, *The Correspondence: 1842–1867,* ed. Edwin Haviland Miller, vol. 1 (New York: New York University Press, 1961), 68.

2. American Battlefield Protection Program, "Fredericksburg I," *CWSAC Battle Summaries,* http://www.nps.gov/hps/abpp/battles/va028.htm.

3. Quoted in Roy Morris Jr., *America's Civil War,* vol. 1 (Leesburg, VA: Empire Press, 1988), 21.

4. "The Fredericksburg Shambles," *Hartford Weekly Times,* December 27, 1862, http://news.google.com/newspapers?nid=2460&dat=18621227 &id=9lE1AAAAIBAJ&sjid=CQAGAAAAIBAJ&pg=6081,7540720.

5. Alexander Hunter, *Johnny Reb and Billy Yank* (New York: Neale Publishing, 1905), 316.

6. Quoted in Robert Roper, *Now the Drum of War: Walt Whitman and His Brothers in the Civil War* (New York: Walker Publishing, 2008), 120.

7. Walt Whitman to Louisa Van Velsor Whitman, *The Correspondence,* 1:59.

8. Walt Whitman, "Our Wounded and Sick Soldiers," *New York Times,* December 11, 1864, http://www.nytimes.com/1864/12/11/news/our-wounded-sick-soldiers-visits-among-army-hospitals-washington-field-here-new.html.

9. Michael Cooper and Dalia Sussman, "Massacre at School Sways Public in Way Earlier Shootings Didn't," *New York Times,* January 17, 2013, http://www.nytimes.com/2013/01/18/us/poll-shows-school-shooting-sways-views-on-guns.html.

10. John Dewey, *The Public and Its Problems,* ed. Melvin L. Rogers (University Park, PA: Pennsylvania State University Press, 2012), 141.

11. Horace Traubel, *With Walt Whitman in Camden,* vol. 6 (Carbondale: Southern Illinois University Press, 1982), 194.

12. Aristotle, *Politics* 1:1253a.

13. Walt Whitman, *Democratic Vistas* (1871; repr., New York: Library of America, 1982), 935.

14. Ibid., 936.

15. Ibid., 990.

16. Ibid.

17. Whitman, *Democratic Vistas: The Original Edition in Facsimile,* ed. Ed Folsom (Iowa City: University of Iowa Press, 2010), 71.

18. Whitman, *Democratic Vistas,* 951.

19. Ibid., 935.

20. See Jonathan Haidt, *The Righteous Mind: Why Good People Are Divided by Religion and Politics* (New York: Penguin, 2012).

21. U.S. Census Bureau, "Voting and Registration in the Election of November 2012," Table 7, http://www.census.gov/hhes/www/socdemo/voting/publications/p20/2012/tables.html.

22. Thomas Carlyle, "Shooting Niagara: And After?," in *Critical and Miscellaneous Essays*, vol. 3 (London: Chapman and Hall, 1888), 596.

23. Ibid.

24. Ibid., 589.

25. Whitman, *Democratic Vistas*, 943.

26. Ibid., 930.

27. Ibid., 937.

28. Ibid.

29. Ibid.

30. Ibid.

31. Ibid., 939.

32. Ibid.

33. Walt Whitman, "Song of Myself" in *Leaves of Grass* (1855; repr., New York: Library of America, 1982), 27.

34. Ibid., 45.

35. Walt Whitman, "Proto-Leaf," in *Selected Poems 1855–1892: A New Edition*, ed. Gary Schmidgall (New York: St. Martin's Press, 1999), 182.

36. Whitman, *Democratic Vistas*, 948.

37. Ibid., 946.

38. Ibid.

39. Ibid., 929.

40. Ibid., 976.

41. Ibid., 977.

42. Walt Whitman, "A Song for Occupations," in *Leaves of Grass*, 93.

43. Whitman, *Democratic Vistas*, 932.

44   Ibid., 989.

45. Ibid., 933.

46. Ibid., 934.

47. Ibid., 955.

48. Ibid., 973.

49. Ibid., 955.

50. Ibid.

51. Ibid.

52. Ibid., 932.

53. Ibid. These ellipses are mine and do indicate omitted words.

54. Ibid.

55. Ibid., 981–82.

56. Ibid., 981.

57. Charles J. Robertson, *Temple of Invention: History of a National Landmark* (London: Scala Publishers, 2006).

58. Walt Whitman, *Memoranda During the War* (Camden, NJ: Author's Publication, 1876–77), 10–11.

59. Walt Whitman, *Notebooks and Unpublished Prose Manuscripts*, ed. Edward F. Grier, vol. 2 (New York: New York University Press, 1984), 520.

60. Walt Whitman, *The Correspondence*, 1:123n76.

61. Whitman, *Memoranda During the War*, 31.

62. Ibid., 13.

63. Ibid., 12.

64. Ibid., 53.

65. Peter Coviello, ed., "Introduction" to *Walt Whitman's Memoranda During the War* (New York: Oxford University Press, 2004), ix–liv.

66. Whitman, *Memoranda During the War*, 50–51.

67. Ibid., 25.

68. Ibid., 29.

69. Ibid., 59.

70. Whitman, *Democratic Vistas*, 946.

71. Walt Whitman to Ralph Waldo Emerson, January 17, 1863, *The Correspondence*, 1:70.

72. Ibid.

73. Walt Whitman, "Vigil Strange I Kept on the Field One Night," in *Selected Poems*, 276–77.

74. Walt Whitman, "Preface, 1876," in *Complete Prose* (1892; repr., New York: Library of America, 1982), 1005.

75. Whitman, *Democratic Vistas*, 982.

76. Michael Ignatieff, *The Needs of Strangers* (New York: Viking, 1985).

77. For something approaching a contemporary version of this thesis, see Danielle S. Allen, *Talking to Strangers: Anxieties of Citizenship since* Brown v. Board of Education (Chicago: University of Chicago Press, 2004).

78. Whitman, "Over the Carnage Rose a Voice Prophetic," 449.

Conclusion: At Whitman's Tomb

Epigraph: Walt Whitman, "Song of Myself," in *Leaves of Grass* (1855; repr., New York: Library of America, 1982), 87.

1.   David S. Reynolds, *Walt Whitman's America: A Cultural Biography* (New York: Alfred A. Knopf, 1995), 588–89.

2.   Ibid., 571–72.

3.   Whitman, "Song of Myself," 88.

4.   Ibid., 32.

5.   Robert Blair, *The Grave: A Poem* (London: Dewick & Clarke, 1806), 13.

6.   Reynolds, *Walt Whitman's America*, 529.

7.   Benton H. Wilson to Walt Whitman, December 27, 1868, Walt Whitman Archive, http://www.whitmanarchive.org/biography/correspondence/reconstruction/tei/loc.01995.html.

8.   Quoted in Roy Morris Jr., *The Better Angel: Walt Whitman in the Civil War* (New York: Oxford University Press, 2000), 236.

9.   Walt Whitman to Susan Stafford, May 28, 1887, *The Correspondence: 1842–1867*, ed. Edwin Haviland Miller, vol. 4 (New York: New York University Press, 1969), 94–95.

10. Joann P. Krieg, "Fritzinger, Frederick Warren (1866–1899)," *Walt Whitman: An Encyclopedia*, ed. J. R. LeMaster and Donald D. Kummings (New York: Garland Publishing, 1998), 240.

11. Todd S. Purdum, "Walt Rostow, Adviser to Kennedy and Johnson, Dies at 86," *New York Times*, February 15, 2003, http://www.nytimes.com/2003/02/15/obituaries/15ROST.html.

12. Michael Schulman, "Family Visit," *The New Yorker* 15 April 2013, 24–25.

13. Ralph Waldo Emerson, quoted in George Searle Phillips, "Walt Whitman," *New-York Illustrated News* 2 (1860): 60, http://www.whitmanarchive.org/criticism/reviews/leaves1860/anc.00038.html.

14. Lewis Hyde, *The Gift: Imagination and the Erotic Life of Property* (New York: Vintage Books, 1983), xvii.

15. Whitman, "Song of Myself," 72.